rediscovering the
Father-heart of God

rediscovering the
Father-heart of God

JEFF LUCAS

crossway books

CROSSWAY BOOKS
38 De Montfort Street, Leicester LE1 7GP, England

First published 1991 under the title Sweet and Sour Pork
Second edition 1997

British Library Cataloguing in Publication Data
A catalogue record for this book is available from the British
Library.

ISBN 1–85684–127–8

Set in Palatino

Typeset in Great Britain by Parker Typesetting Service,
Leicester

Printed in Great Britain
by The Guernsey Press Company Limited,
Guernsey, Channel Islands

To my frequent flier family:
Kay, Kelly and Richard

Contents

Foreword

When Jeff announced his intention to write something I was thrilled. How useful literacy would be to him in his leadership role, I reflected, and how I looked forward to receiving his first genuine attempt at letter-writing after all those years of crude Letraset epistles with the big cross in the bottom right-hand corner.

When, however, I learned that my (erstwhile) friend was planning to publish a book which sought to transmit divine truths through the medium of humour, I felt deeply troubled in my spirit. I was already aware of areas of tension between us.

He attends the type of church whose people feel that 'liturgy' is something you collect from the Indian takeaway. Who am I to criticize? They organize their spontaneity so much more effectively than Mother Carey's chickens, of which I am one.

We use different versions of the Bible. Jeff favours the 'Living, throbbing, slides along the pew, opens itself at random and points out a verse meant specially for you' version. I use a version that is re-punctuated and privately printed by a group of people who eschew excessive use of the colon. Does it matter? I know a man whose life was transformed by an apostrophe in Leviticus.

I toil with a spade in my garden. Jeff stands Mike Morris on the vegetable patch and sings choruses at him.

None of these differences would have mattered. We could have coped somehow.

But for Jeff to write a warm, humorous, helpful book about the fatherly love of God, parts of which made me laugh out loud, seems to me an act of deepest treachery. Jeff is a fine preacher, but preachers are not supposed to make the transition to writing with such ease and proficiency. If he starts producing books that are funnier than mine, I shall smash his head in – in love.

Besides, if too many people get the message that God really does love them, they'll all get converted and we'll both be out of a job.

Wise up, Jeff! Cut out the entertainment, the humour, the accessibly conversational tone, vulgarly obvious honesty and the sense of God's extravagant goodwill that pervades the book. That'll put you back in the mainstream of Christian literature.

Cheers, mate!

Adrian Plass

Introduction

Now don't misunderstand me. It's not that I'm some kind of heavy-duty doubter. It's just that there are times when it seems that God is speaking to me . . . but then again, I'm not so sure.

Do you ever feel like that? You hear those gloriously bionic testimonies of how God converses with some people 20,000 times before breakfast, but somehow when it comes down to the issue of you hearing from God, particularly in a moment of pressure, it doesn't always seem quite so simple.

That's how I felt that wet, windy Saturday afternoon when I sensed the Lord say: 'Tonight I will teach you a lesson that you will never forget.'

As the words circled persistently around my brain, I speculated about their source. Was this the voice of the eternal God . . . or the whispering of the devil . . . or the after-effects of last night's pizza?

The thought returned again, more forcefully now, and brought with it a growing sense of excitement and anticipation. As I sloshed my way across the waterlogged sports field, vainly trying to fight off the English monsoon with my umbrella, I decided: this must be the Lord.

11

Now you may well be wondering what on earth I was doing walking on a flooded soccer pitch conversing with the Creator. The occasion was an event called Solid Ground (not a very prophetic title that, I thought, as I squished my way through the muddy mess underfoot), a weekend of celebration and Bible teaching held at the national headquarters of British Youth For Christ in the English Midlands.

The meetings were being held in a huge tent. As I rushed in out of the downpour, the worship band was already playing, and about 700 damp, tired but enthusiastic young people were parked on blankets and groundsheets. I headed towards the makeshift platform, sat on a box out of the way and opened my soggy notes. Just time for a last-minute check through my prepared scribble.

My brief for the evening was to deliver a talk on 'The power of the Holy Spirit'. A thousand thoughts race through a preacher's brain just prior to speaking. 'Will they listen?' 'Are the youth leaders here open to a charismatic experience?' 'Will God turn up at the end of the talk and obligingly fill people with his power?'

It was time for the talk. The worship had been bright and bouncy, and I walked on to the platform and invited Richard, our four-year-old son, to join me. Richard was there for a specific purpose. I wanted to use our father-son relationship as an illustration of God's heart for his children. Power alone can be frightening. I've met many Christians who really want to experience a greater dimension of the Holy Spirit, but they're terrified of the so-called 'Holy Ghost'. Inadequate teaching has caused many to view a charismatic experience as something akin to a spiritual mugging. The Holy Spirit becomes a heavenly electrical charge rather than a person; 'it' instead of 'he'. It's not surprising that fear develops when an encounter with the Third Person of the Trinity is seen as the spiritual equivalent to putting your fingers into a power socket.

So I walked to the microphone, and lifted Richard into my arms. My words were deliberate, the illustration was simple and obvious: 'I want you all to meet Richard, my little boy.'

On cue, 700 voices said, 'Hi, Richard.' A few girls sighed and said, 'Oh, he's so cute.' I began to feel quite flattered and then realized they were talking about my son.

'Now I love my son a lot,' I continued. 'And I love to do him good, and I wouldn't dream of giving him anything that would hurt or destroy him. Even when I discipline him it's because I love him. He's safe with me. In fact, if a choice had to be made between my life and his, I'd die for him without hesitation. Why? It's simple. I'm his daddy.'

I paused for a moment and looked at the sea of faces. There were some misty eyes and a tear glistened here and there, but this was more than a display of self-indulgent sentimentality on my part. I had to communicate the truth that the power of God comes from the heart and hands of a loving heavenly Father. God is Dad, not a heavenly nuclear reactor. He comes to embrace us, not just turbo-charge us. We relax in the potential of the supernatural when we understand it in the context of fatherhood.

Richard looked at me as I continued. 'So please understand that you have nothing to fear. Look at me as I hold my son, and know that God who is your Father loves you a billion times more than I can love Richard. He is the One who goes beyond saying, "I'd lay down my life for you." Jesus is able to say, "I *have* laid down my life for you." So relax. It's all right. Daddy's here.'

And that was supposed to be the end of my little illustration. Richard would toddle back to my wife, Kay, who was waiting at the side of the platform, I'd open my Bible, teach, and then we'd pray, and minister to people.

That was the plan. But God had said, 'Tonight I'll teach you a lesson that you'll never forget.' Time for school.

Suddenly, Richard leaned back in my arms and opened his arms wide. At first I thought he was going to give me a playful punch, which would have utterly wrecked the illustration (demonstration of warm relationship destroyed by Father holding handkerchief to profusely bleeding nose). But instead he wrapped his arms tightly around my neck and buried his face in my shoulder like he never wanted to let go. We stood there for a few seconds. No movement or words, just a simple, silent parable of Father and Son.

Suddenly, school began as the Holy Spirit fell upon that crowd. Immediately, there was commotion all over the place. People speaking in languages that they'd never learned. I heard the sound of laughing and giggling because they'd never heard themselves do that before. A few demons making their presence felt with the odd scream here and there. Bodies collapsing under the power of God. A sovereign move of God broke out, so powerful that in the next twenty minutes, as people came into the tent, they could immediately sense the raw power of God. A number of people marched up to the platform because at the moment when the Spirit of God ignited the place, they had been instantly healed.

And all the time I just stood there, holding my son tightly in my arms. Noel Richards and the worship band played quietly. What do you do when God arrives?

Well, sadly, if you're a leader, you often feel obliged to do something, which in retrospect seems absurd. Looking back on it now it was ludicrous, but you have to understand – I'd been asked to speak, so I felt like I *had* to speak! After about twenty minutes of just standing there watching the Lord at work, I sent Richard back to Kay, opened my Bible and started my talk. It was impossible! Ever tried explaining the work of the Holy Spirit when the Holy Spirit is working overtime? More people were being filled with power, a few more demons were doing their little Alsatian impersonations . . . so after about ten minutes I gave up, closed my Bible and just enjoyed the view. It was the shortest message I had ever preached. (In fact, when the organizers of the weekend sent me an honorarium for my ministry, they included a sum of money for Richard, on the basis that he did more on the Saturday night than I did.)

'Tonight I'll teach you a lesson . . .' God was showing me a simple, powerful principle, so obvious yet so overlooked. *People need to know him as Father*.

When we wake up to the reality that the God of the universe wants to father us, there will be a revolution in our lives; a concrete sense of safety that causes us to be at home with the supernatural; a rising surge of gratitude that will motivate creative service; a growing call to intimacy that will deliver us from cold religion.

A little boy hugged his dad. The people not only saw

it, but understood in that moment something of God's heart for them, and in that second a measure of fullness was released.

People need to know God as Father. That's why the Lord Jesus came to this planet and talked continuously about his Father. Other religious teachers had come and gone with their debates about morality, philosophy and law. But Jesus was different. He *did* talk about sin; he *did* point a prophetic finger in the Pharisees' direction and expose mere religion; but more than that, he came to paint a portrait of Father God.

As part of that mission, Jesus told a story that we commonly know as the parable of the Prodigal Son (recorded in Luke 15:11–32). He had a mixed bag of listeners that day: pompous Pharisees bedecked in their finery preened themselves on the edge of the crowd, self-assured smiles on their faces, whispering behind cupped hands. Mothers with children frowned at the brassy prostitutes who squealed at each other's old jokes. The curious mingled with the confused. Some were the life and soul, some were lonely, some were respected, some were considered dregs, but all were orphans before God. So Jesus told them a story which had a simple plot and three major characters: a crazy mixed-up Jewish kid who fled the family home in search of the bright lights; the Prodigal's elder brother, a nice guy who never left home but whose heart was with the pigs all along; and the father of them both.

As the crowds listened, they met themselves. The 'sinners' wept as they heard of the utter depravity of this Jewish boy wishing his father dead, and then eating with pigs. The pharisaic experts shuffled uncomfortably when the self-righteous elder brother was brought on

16

stage, religion personified. Everyone looked in a mirror that day as Jesus spoke.

But the Christian gospel is more than a message to convict the sinful and to humble the religious. Christianity is at heart the good news about who God is.

So Jesus introduces the third character, the father, and as he does so he paints a vivid portrait of contrast. The father's character is displayed against the dull and muddy backdrop of sinful rebellion and stern religion, and so he shines even brighter.

In this most beautiful story, Jesus shows us the hopeless futility of life without God, and of religion without God. Then having shown us all what we are like at both our best and our worst, he effectively declares, 'Now meet my Father.'

I have travelled many thousands of miles to preach and teach since that night at Solid Ground, and I am even more convinced today that Christians need to have a greater understanding of three primary truths.

First, we must see the 'sinfulness of sin'. Here the Prodigal Son himself can teach us.

Second, we must see that religiosity is the primary temptation to those who mean business with the living God. We must expose it and avoid it at all cost. Here the elder brother can teach us.

Third, and most important, we must have a heart-revelation of this God who insists that we call him 'Abba' – Daddy – and here of course we can glean a great deal from the father character in the parable.

As we look together at this story, I pray that you will feel the embrace of God afresh.

I

THE SON

chapter one

'Gimme that thing!'

Two seconds ago he was a man asleep in bed, but now, as the funky music plays, his eyes flash open, blue and bright. The first expression on his waking face is a gleaming smile. Hurling the crisp white sheets back, he does a triple backflip out of the bed, landing squarely on his feet, a picture of health and perfection. He's been asleep for eight hours, but his hair is perfectly in place, his pyjamas pressed with cavalry precise creases. Suddenly, his Miss World wife and Waltons children dance into the room, all smiles and cornflakes, and thus the source of their joy is revealed, for they start their day with *cornflakes*. Together the family unite in a stirring anthem that celebrates the attributes of this most marvellous breakfast cereal. As the commercial concludes, we have a frozen family shot: Mum and Dad are smiling, the two kids are smiling, the dog and the pet boa constrictor are smiling – and all because of cornflakes.

We don't sing about cereal in our house. That isn't to say that we don't enjoy a nice bowl of cornflakes, but we don't serenade the packet.

Come to think of it, there are lots of things that those TV commercial families do that seem a million miles from reality. I like chocolate – particularly that chocolate with the coconut inside. There is, however, a problem in that when I take a bite of the aforementioned confectionery, for some reason I don't find myself standing on an exotic South Pacific beach in the shade of a palm tree.

Do you remember that commercial for Hai Karate aftershave? It featured a rather substantial woman who looked like Arnold Schwarzenegger in a bikini. I used to like that aftershave and wore it daily for a number of years, but never once can I recall any bikini-clad ladies drop-kicking and karate-chopping anybody or anything in order to get their hands on me.

And in our house, Mother doesn't stand by the sink gently extolling the virtues of the washing-up liquid while the rest of us hum a little song about the green stuff, whereupon Mum shows us just how soft her hands are. In our house, Mum is more likely to be growling about how hard her hands can be when applied to the backsides of those blighters who don't help with the dishes.

Advertising executives have created a very attractive world that doesn't actually exist. It's a strange place, where teapots dance when you put a certain brand of teabag in them, and where only one beer can reach the parts that others find unreachable. Life, unlike the movies, doesn't come with backing music.

But despite the funny and often fantastic elements of television advertising, generally speaking you will find a clear message in every commercial, whatever the product. They all announce that we can be happy . . . *if*. If we have this aftershave, that car, this food, that holiday, this pair of jeans, that drink, this house and, indeed, that breakfast cereal.

It's appealing stuff, because most of us want to be happy. Ask the average beauty contestant what she wants to do with her life and she'll most likely tell you that she wants to help the poor, travel widely, do a day-release programme with Mother Teresa and, 'Well, I want to be happy in my life.'

Years ago, the pop song 'Don't worry, be happy' was so successful that George Bush adopted it as his presidential campaign theme. Hardly a masterpiece of musical brilliance, the song appealed to the desire in all of us to be able to have a more joyous existence on this planet.

And happiness is not frowned on by God. I make every attempt to avoid those Christians who seem to equate holiness with a lack-lustre approach to life, and wear a facial expression usually associated with severe constipation. Miseries can be found scattered in almost any church congregation on a Sunday morning. Arms folded, faces fixed in a firm 'bless me if you dare' expression, these Lazarus look-alikes seem to revel in joyless religion. For them, 'happy' is a filthy word, and fun of any kind, however clean, is tantamount to blasphemy. Many Christians feel comfortable with tears, and nervous with laughter.

Of course we want to experience real happiness. But tonight, and every night, the world's televisions will proclaim that happiness is indeed available, but on one condition – that you buy what's being sold. And it seems that the evangelists of consumerism are making believers out of us, for as one writer put it: 'Contemporary culture is plagued by the passion to possess.'[1] I saw a

23

slogan on a T-shirt which sums up the consumer gospel: 'Life is a game. Whoever ends up with the most toys wins.' In Britain, millions sit spellbound every Saturday hoping that the silvery National Lottery finger of luck will point at them: 'It could be you!'

We breathlessly charge through our lives, frantically grabbing armfuls of items as we go, but we feel strangely empty even as we accumulate.

> There was a man who had two sons . . . The younger one said to his father, 'Father, give me my share of the estate.'

Now it goes without saying that the Prodigal never saw any TV commercials. Nevertheless he very definitely believed in the 'Get things – get happy' philosophy of life, and would have worn that T-shirt with pride in his early days. That's why he left home in the first place. It wasn't as if he had nothing: in fact, the opposite is true. The family that Jesus describes seems to be quite wealthy. The narrative talks about servants, fatted calves, robes and rings, and describes a father who is able to give his son an inheritance in hard cash. This household was a long way from the breadline: so why leave?

The answer is quite simple, really, and it can all be summed up in two words: 'Give me.' Even though he had enjoyed plenty, the boy felt that it just wasn't enough for his appetites. He had an abundance, but he wanted more. He'd spent hours daydreaming about what life would be like if he could have more, until, finally, he could stand it no longer.

By Jewish law, an inheritance could be given prior to death, but the capital would be kept by the giver until his demise. Only the *interest* on the capital would be immediately available to the beneficiary. But the Prodigal didn't ask for the interest – he wanted his whole inheritance then and there. In other words, he was acting as if his dad had died. He knew that his father would be mortally wounded.

'Dad, I can't wait. I really want to live while I'm still young. *Give me my share!*'

The long pathway to his personal hell began – not with a murder or a bank robbery – but when he decided to adopt 'I want to be happy, so give me' as his slogan for living. *Discontent* drove him out into the lonely cold.

Before we investigate the parable any further, we need to ask ourselves: have we been brainwashed by the 'Give me things, give me happiness' message?

Perhaps you've never faced that question before, because it's so difficult to develop a balanced view on the issue. On the one hand, some sections of the church (particularly in the USA) preach a 'Jesus wants you to be rich' prosperity gospel, while others go to the other extreme and seem to preach a 've haf vays of making you sell your car, buy Oxfam clothes and ride a rusty bike in Jesus' name' poverty gospel.

Blessed are the rich . . .

One of the leading lights of the American faith/prosperity movement is convinced that Jesus appeared to him in a hospital ward and announced, 'If my children listen to me, I will make them wealthy.'[2]

Another nationally known preacher, who leads a church with a 20,000-strong congregation, says that 'God doesn't mind if we have five Cadillacs or a

25

Cadillac, Mercedes and a Rolls Royce all thrown in the same bag'.[3] What fantastic news for the greedy! Now we pious prodigals can say 'Give me', and do it in Jesus' name! As we cruise past a street person in our luxuriously appointed new car (which the Lord blessed me with, isn't he just so good?), we can be pleased that it's just another fruit of faith-filled living. Instead of exposing and confronting greed, some have sanctified it, as they present a cosmetically changed Jesus who will make all our wildest dreams come true. Some teachers have suggested that Jesus only wanted the millionaire rich young ruler to give away his money so that he could become a billionaire as a result! Greed becomes a creed.

Blessed are they that are paid peanuts . . .

Of course, the other extreme attitude to the material is just as dangerous. The prosperity gospel is rooted in the American culture, and the poverty gospel is clearly British! Church leaders are often paid a pittance because 'it's for the kingdom'. During an induction service for a new minister, one of the deacons stood to his feet and prayed, 'Lord, you keep this man humble; we'll keep him poor!' The absurd notion is that anointing and cash are incompatible, because money is 'unspiritual'. Perhaps that's why some churches seem to be living on another planet when it comes to paying guest speakers.

Perhaps, like me, you find yourself in the middle of the two extremes. You don't want to drive a Rolls Royce, but you're not convinced that a bike or, worse, a Reliant Robin is the way forward either! You're not comfortable with extravagance, but you don't want to hang Tear

Fund teabags on the washing line so that you can use them a second time round. (A friend of mine made a spoof appeal at a large Christian event for used teabags to be donated for the missionaries. She was inundated with them; gifts from well-meaning folk who took her seriously.)

The antidote to consumerism: contentment

I'd like to suggest that we can avoid the pigpen trail as we learn to live in an attitude of contentment. When the kingdom of God truly comes in our lives, the driving need to accumulate goes. Contentment is a sign that the kingdom has come to us. That's why John the Baptist counselled the soldiers who found faith to walk in financial integrity and be content with their pay.[4] This kingdom attitude is a million miles from an insular 'I'm all right, Jack' kind of contentment where, like fat cats full of cream, we care only that we are warm and well-fed. Rather, it is rooted in thankfulness, joyful generosity and sacrificial giving. Perhaps the best way to illustrate the principle is to look at one individual who lived the concept.

A model of contentment: Paul

If the prosperity preachers are right, and all Christians can expect a five-star Hilton lifestyle, then Paul must have been seriously backslidden! While there were times when he enjoyed a healthy bank balance ('I know what it is to have plenty'),[5] he also received a few bills printed in red ink ('I know what it is to be in need'). Through all the financial ups and downs, however, Paul is able to write to his friends at Philippi: 'I have learned the secret of being content in any and every situation, whether well fed or hungry, whether living in plenty or in want. I can do everything through him who gives me strength.'[6]

These amazing words were spoken by a man who clearly had his feet on the ground when it came to financial matters. Paul was no ethereal 'space cadet' who was too spiritual to be practical ('I don't need money, I eat manna for breakfast'). He knew that Christians, like all human beings, need cash to live, and so he was openly grateful to those who financially supported his ministry,[7] and was the author of a systematic plan to raise finance for Christians in need.[8] He worked out his faith in the real world.

Paul had come to view money as his servant – he was not the servant of money. He learned to live a positive life which no longer depended on a positive cashflow. Contentment was his, whatever the rate of inflation.

Writing to a young leader he declared: 'Godliness with contentment is great gain.'[9] Simplified, his argument goes something like this: The financially rich aren't really rich. Those who are contented are the real millionaires, whatever the state of their bank balance.

Contentment is the key to a successful life on this prodigal planet. But it's an attitude that we *learn*; it doesn't come naturally. Part of the learning process is to identify and expose a few myths.

Major myth no. 1: money makes you happier

The Bible isn't against wealth. Loving money not cash itself, is the root of all evil.[10] There were obviously some wealthy people in the early church. That's why instruction was given that the more affluent shouldn't be treated with favouritism;[11] that they should make sure their trust was in God,[12] not in their savings, and that they should be generous.[13]

Scripture clearly speaks out, however, against the notion that money will bring happiness. While I don't want to suggest that those wealthier than you and me are all rampant depressives, the truth remains that the 'good life' provides no lasting guarantee of happiness.

Where are they now?

In 1923, a 'think tank' meeting to plan and strategize America's economic future was held at the Edgewater Hotel in Chicago, Illinois. Nine of the richest and most powerful businessmen and politicians were invited to take part. Alongside the head of the New York Stock Exchange sat Wall Street's top stockbroker. The presidents of the nation's largest independent steel, utility and oil companies were there. The head of the world's largest corporate monopoly, the nation's most successful wheat speculator, the president of the International Bank of Settlements, and a member of the US Presidential Cabinet sat together around that auspicious table that day. It was certainly an impressive cast list: these men were fabulously wealthy and held incredible power and influence at a national and international level. They lived lives that most people dream of, at the very pinnacle of their chosen professions. Surely such success would bring lifelong satisfaction?

So what happened to these high-fliers? Thirty years later, the picture wasn't nearly so rosy.

Charles Schwann, the steel-company chief, died bankrupt, his last five years spent as a chronic depressive with weekly visits to his psychiatrist. Howard Hobson, the oil magnate, died insane in a mental asylum. The head of the corporate monopoly, committed suicide, as did the President of the International Bank of Settlements. Jesse Livermore, famous top Wall Street broker, also killed himself. Samuel Insell (head of the utility company), Richard Whitney (head of the New York Stock Exchange) and Arthur Cruton (the great wheat speculator) all got into trouble with the law. Insell and Cruton died as fugitives abroad, on the run from the police; Whitney spent a lengthy term in Sing Sing Prison and died bankrupt. Finally, Albert Fulwell, the Presidential Cabinet member, was pardoned from prison so that he could die at home, eaten up with disease.

Riches and prestige guaranteed nothing for those men. They were comfortable but dissatisfied. Why?

Surely Jesus gives the answer to that question: 'A man's life does not consist in the abundance of his possessions.'[14] Luke 12:15

Stop! Read those words again. In fact, why not read them a dozen times or so. I wish that we could print that scripture on every university degree, on every stock certificate, on every payslip and on every banknote. Maybe we could print those words on huge banners and hang them prominently in every shopping centre, especially during the frantic January sales, when hoards of mutant ninja consumers fight to the death for a deal! The truth must get out: while 'things' are nice, they will never provide a lasting sense of satisfaction. Yes, that new car *will* make you feel quite jolly for a while, but it won't be very long (days or weeks rather than months or years) before the buzz wears off.

Of course, we don't want to believe the truth. Some people would be devastated to discover this news,

30

because if money won't ultimately bring happiness, what else is there? We prefer to say, 'Well, it may be true, but I want to find out for myself – gimme!' Time to look at another Bible character . . .

Solomon really did have it all. An Old Testament billionaire, he decided to conduct an important experiment. The subject of his test was simply, 'Where can I find happiness?' Being one of the richest men in the world, he spared no expense in his search. He tried everything. The best vintage wines were brought from the royal cellars and the king partied! He drank so much that he acted like a fool.[15] He got a king-sized headache, but he didn't get happy.

Then he turned his attention to releasing his creative streak. (How many of us have dreamed of being able to buy a cottage on a remote sun-kissed beach where we could make pottery all day to the sound of the breaking surf?) He built houses and reservoirs, he planted vineyards and gardens and parks. He threw himself into accumulation with a passion, ultimately becoming the richest king in the nation's history.[16] Surely happiness and fulfilment came to a man so wealthy?

Wrong! Listen to some of the words and phrases this billionaire uses to describe his feelings: 'Meaningless . . . chasing after the wind . . . vanity . . . I hated life.' Can you hear his voice of warning ringing down through the years? Solomon had it all and did it all, and his advice is: 'Don't bother – it's a waste of space. Believe me – I know.'

Wake up and expose the myth now, because in the rat race there are no winners.

Major myth no. 2: when my circumstances are more pleasant, contentment will come

Florida's Disneyland has a time-travel ride which takes you through robotically simulated scenes of domestic life over the last 100 years. Looking back, you wonder how people lived without the modern conveniences that we take for granted. How strange to have to pump your water rather than turn on a tap! The phonograph sounds so scratchy. What did they do without radio or television?

What really caught my attention, however, was the song that is played in the background as you travel through each different decade. The words are simple: 'Now is the time, now is the best time, now is the best time of your life.'

As the ride finished, I asked myself: am I living life with joy and contentment in the here and now, or am I waiting for some better circumstances to arrive and *then* I'll be happy? Do I treat *now*, even if 'now' is dark with pain, as the best time of my life? Or does Paul Tournier's description of humanity fit me? 'Most people spend their entire life indefinitely preparing to live.'[17]

Some people live for years on a psychological location known as Someday Isle. 'Some day I'll be happy . . . when I've left school/left college/got married/had children/when the children leave home/when I get divorced/when I retire . . .'

For years we look upon happiness in the future tense: 'There are better times ahead.' Unfortunately, happiness always seems to be on the horizon; we get older, but never any closer to that elusive joy. In the meantime, great chunks of life are wasted. Finally, we arrive at old age, rather embittered and cynical and by now bored and disillusioned with Someday Isle. It's time for a change, so we mentally relocate to Memory Lane. 'Do you remember that Christmas when all the children were still at home? Ah, those were the days. We had a great time, didn't we? They were the best days of our lives.'

Actually, they were *not* the best days at all, because we were living on Someday Isle back then. Still, those who live on Memory Lane don't have the most accurate of memories.

Contrast that with the attitude of a young Jewish girl, who wrote this poem while surrounded by the horrors of a Nazi concentration camp:

> From tomorrow on
> I shall be sad
> From tomorrow on
> Not today
> Today I will be glad
> And every day
> No matter how bitter it may be
> I shall say
> From tomorrow on I shall be sad
> Not today.

One writer points out that we, surrounded by relative luxury, have rewritten the poem:

> From tomorrow on
> I shall be happy
> From tomorrow on
> Not today

Today I will be sad
And every day
No matter how good things may be
I shall say
From tomorrow on I'll be happy
Not today.[18]

The fact is that contentment isn't based on the right set
of circumstances. For one reason, it's quite difficult to
get the circumstances of our lives fine-tuned enough to
be that consistently pleasant. I don't want to sound as
though I have a jaundiced approach to life, but have you
noticed how even the exciting bits never quite turn out
to be as good as you'd hoped? You spend weeks
planning that big family holiday abroad, and pore over
those glossy brochures full of impossibly good-looking
holidaymakers. The hotel looks wonderful, the sea a
deep blue. This is going to be the greatest holiday of
your entire life.

On the way to the airport, however, your child throws
up on the back seat, and this is just the beginning of your
sorrows. The flight attendant on the plane treats you like
a stray donkey and serves you a plate that looks like an
aeriel view of a farmyard. When you finally arrive, the
hotel is nice, but you have been given a room next to a
group of forty-seven rabid party animals who are
attempting to get their names listed in the *Guinness
Book of Records* for drinking the most beer in the least
time!

For some reason life is not like the brochures. Even the
more simple 'joyful' moments don't always work out as
planned.

A few months ago I decided to do my bit as an

enthusiastic family person. 'Let's all go out for a picnic,' I cried jubilantly, totally forgetting that a gale was blowing outside. Immediately my hyperactive imagination was filled with thoughts of warm family togetherness. The children would play contentedly on the swings, while Kay and I enjoyed our sandwiches and cakes, luxuriously lying with the warmth of the sun on our backs, the balmy English countryside rolling before us . . .

What *actually* happened was that my wife and two close family friends (they must be close and committed to us to picnic with us during a gale) sat huddled and shivering beneath blankets nibbling damp sandwiches, while the children fought over the solitary swing. You couldn't see the balmy rolling countryside because of the balmy rolling fog.

That's life, but even if your circumstances are temporarily quite perfect, ultimate contentment won't come.

Not convinced? Let's go back to that chap Solomon again. He had enough money to make sure that all the little mundane and boring bits of his life were removed. He hired hundreds of servants to do all the tedious things for him. From his waking moment until his eyelids closed at night, he was served. Just imagine it: a cup of tea and cooked breakfast when you wake up; stepping out of the bath that someone else ran for you, you hold out your arms and yet another servant dresses you in your immaculately cleaned and pressed designer clothes. In your life, washing-up doesn't exist. There is no vacuuming. Someone else is cleaning the car. All you have to do is have fun – and with money to burn, the sky's the limit!

Then Solomon took things further. He decided to explore and express his sexuality. Casting any sense of morality to the wind, this Old Testament stud made James Bond look like the Singing Nun! Seven hundred wives!

What unregenerate male hasn't dreamed of being able to snap his fingers and cause the ladies to come running, especially after watching Cruise or Selleck in action on the silver screen? Solomon lived out that sexual fantasy. The ultimate hedonist, he even employed a full-time group of singers and musicians to serenade him on command.

Well, come on, Solomon, what was it like? You lived a dream: tell us about it!

The reply may surprise us. 'Meaningless! . . . Everything is meaningless!'[19] The man had everything – and had nothing.

Think of Paul again, who had nothing – but everything. He wrote those words about contentment from a prison cell, on what could have been death row for all he knew. He'd had some really rough times since finding faith:

I have worked much harder, been in prison more frequently, been flogged more severely, and been exposed to death again and again. Five times I received from the Jews the forty lashes minus one. Three times I was beaten with rods, once I was stoned, three times I was shipwrecked, I spent a night and a day in the open sea . . . I have been in danger from rivers . . . from bandits . . . from my own countrymen . . . from Gentiles; in danger in the city . . . in the country . . . at sea; and . . . from false brothers . . . I have known hunger and thirst and have often gone without food; I have been cold and naked.[20]

Jesus wants me for a rich kid? Follow Christ and say goodbye to tribulation? Hardly! What an incredible contrast between the lifestyles of Solomon and Paul! So how on earth is it that Paul is the man with a contented heart?

is not sth that comes naturally
— has to be
learned! ↓

Paul's secret: Jesus

'I have learned the (secret) of being content in any and every situation . . . I can do everything through him who gives me strength.'[21]

If it wasn't for the fact that I'm quoting Scripture, I'd be tempted to apologize for sounding a little trite and simplistic. But Paul doesn't need a 500-page book to explain the source of his strength. He says it like this: 'I'm contented because of Jesus Christ.'

His life has been stripped down to the starkest minimum: all he really has is his next breath, and death row may steal even that from him. Everything is all wrong. But everything is all right, because he has a friendship with a God who is bigger than life and death.

Throughout the pages of Scripture God repeatedly tells nervous men and women that everything is OK, just because he is with them.

Moses was terrified at the thought of having to lead the Hebrews out of Egypt, and begged God to send someone else. The Lord had a short answer: 'I will be with you.'[22]

Joshua and Jeremiah heard the same. Joshua was so frightened that God had to repeat the statement three times before it sank in, but the heart of the message was the same: 'I am with you.'[23]

After three years of companionship and teaching,

what were the final words that Jesus spoke to his shivering disciples before he ascended to heaven? 'Surely I am with you always, to the very end of the age.'[24]

Scripture is teaching us that as we make God the central focus of our lives, then his peace and contentment will be ours. That's why we don't have to throw ourselves towards the pig farm with the Prodigal.

The writer to the Hebrews puts it like this: 'Keep your lives free from the love of money and be content with what you have, because God has said, "Never will I leave you; never will I forsake you."'[25] Heb 13:5

With us . . . now

There's a Christian version of the Someday Isle/Memory Lane trip. We can get caught up with the fact that we are people in a process. We want to grow, meet goals, fulfil vision, develop spiritual muscle. We're going for it! While all that is vitally true (most of us need to be more goal-orientated), it's good to remember that *right now* God likes us, and is involved in our lives. Yes, this moment!

Writer Tim Hansel once received a letter from a friend that sums up the nowness of our friendship with God. While it is a little overstated, it illustrates the point.

We have an idea that God is leading us to a desired goal – he is not. His purpose is that I can depend on him and his power now. If I can stay in the middle of the turmoil, calm and unperplexed, that is the end of God's purpose. God's training is for now. This minute . . . when we realise that obedience is the end, then each moment is precious.[26]

That sounds too simplistic!

The post-yuppie generation has a thirst for innovative, complex answers, the more bizarre the better. That's why New Age writers like Shirley MacLaine have become so popular. We like *complicated* answers: they appeal to our sense of intellect.

I learned just how much we complicate our lives during a recent snowfall in Britain. We borrowed a sledge and took to the hills. A few thousand other people had decided to do the same thing, and most of them had the right equipment for riding down snow-covered gradients: a sledge. Some, however, didn't have sledges.

It was fascinating to watch. One man wrapped himself in a groundsheet and shunted himself down the slope, pushing furiously with his elbows; a ruptured eagle came to mind as I watched him. A number were armed with biscuit tins. It was hilarious to see grown and hopefully intelligent men frantically trying to squeeze their buttocks into rather small tins. Some managed to accomplish this, though we wondered whether they would be condemned to live the rest of their lives with a Huntley and Palmer box on their rear ends due to the tightness of the fit. Then they set off on what looked to be an excruciatingly painful downhill journey.

Four men clung to each other and rolled downhill in a plastic sheet, and went sailing straight through a barbed-wire fence! Fortunately, no-one was hurt.

As I watched all this, it occurred to me: don't people make life complicated? Even having fun became an exhausting and dangerous exercise – all because they just didn't have the right equipment.

Perhaps you're not a committed Christian, and you're hunting for contentment through the good life. Maybe you've known what it is to walk with Jesus Christ, but now other ambitions are driving.

Stop now. Hear this Jesus who says, 'Apart from me you can do nothing.'[27] John 15:5

He is the right equipment for life – not just for heaven when you die, but for life and health and laughter and contentment right now. I know it sounds too simple, but it's true. He invites us to put his kingdom first,[28] and to share our needs with him each day;[29] to give generously and cheerfully (the actual word means hysterically),[30] and thereafter laugh all the way *from* the bank – not *to* it. He calls us to find out for ourselves that giving really is better than getting.[31] He invites us to submit our ambitions to him, and to be a people led by him, not driven by our own self-obsessions; to learn persistent gratitude and thanksgiving, refusing to accept popular myths as our philosophy of life.

He offers us contentment, not through a principle or a concept, but through himself. As Tim Hansel puts it: 'The world today says, "Enough is not enough!" Christ answers softly, "Enough is enough." '[32]

Contentment will not come easily. I have probably raised more questions than answers in this chapter. As we continue to study the parable, I hope that you'll find some further signposts towards contentment along the way – particularly as we look at the nature of Father God. But I don't want to give a false impression, like one of those books with the title, '77 Ways Beginning with Z to find Peace, Joy and Contentment Without Really Trying'. Life lessons aren't learned overnight. We will need to allow Jesus to deprogramme our minds and teach us his better way. But God is looking for a people who will enrol in his school of contentment, and who, like Paul, will be prepared to learn.

The door slammed shut behind the Prodigal. Taking one last look back at the warm lights from the house, he turned and walked off into the darkness.

Will we follow in his footsteps?

chapter two

How to avoid
pig farms

Not long after that, the younger son got together all he had, set off for a distant country and there squandered his wealth in wild living. After he had spent everything, there was a severe famine in that whole country, and he began to be in need. So he went and hired himself out to a citizen of that country, who sent him to his fields to feed pigs. He longed to fill his stomach with the pods that the pigs were eating, but no-one gave him anything.

He'd walked about half a mile, and already the bag that was slung across his back was cutting deep into his shoulders. He had promised himself that he wouldn't look back any more. For the last ten minutes he'd been trying to shut out the remembrance of tears rolling down his dad's cheeks. Unable to resist, he stopped and turned around. He could just see the lights of the house in the distance. Was it imagination, or was that his father silhouetted against the light, looking out into certain darkness?

His mind raced. Perhaps it wasn't too late! He could swallow his pride and apologize. But then other thoughts pushed in. He was rich now. Anything he wanted was his for the taking. Think of the excitement, the laughter ahead.

Moving quickly, as if to act before he changed his mind, he adjusted the biting strap, wrapped his cloak more tightly against the night chill, and walked into the dark . . .

The great deception: sin is good for you

I remember an incident that took place when my family and I were on a transatlantic flight. We were 36,000 feet up in the air, halfway across the Atlantic Ocean, and my son (he was only a toddler at the time) was at that stage in life commonly known as 'the terrible twos'. For those who aren't parents, this is that joyous phase that some children go through when behaviour patterns are somewhat modified.

The child *normally* greets his favourite uncle with a hug and a kiss. During this phase, however, the child may well greet that same uncle with a swift kick in the groin, or a playful jab in the solar plexus.

Children going through the terrible twos sit happily on Santa Claus's lap, stick two fingers up his nostrils (all the way to the knuckle) and quietly ask if they can have a Scud missile for Christmas.

Now Richard was not particularly different during this period; I've known some children to develop a serious ministry of devastation, and make the Gaderene demoniac look like the choirboy of the year. It was just that he was restless. So he decided to try to open the emergency exit of the plane. Why not indeed? He was bored. The movie was of no interest to him, and the food had been lovingly prepared by demonized chefs, so he decided to open that door.

Now I'm no aviation expert, but I know that this is not a good idea. The airlines tend to agree, which is why they paint the emergency door handle a lurid shade of red, and print warnings in large letters all around the offending door handle. 'Danger!' screamed the notice. 'Emergency only.' The airline had also thoughtfully written 'Achtung' for the benefit of German toddlers. All of which did nothing to deter my son. He put his hand on the handle. I decided that it would be appropriate for me to intervene.

'Darling, don't touch that door, please!'

My son looked at me, and asked me that question that little boys just love to ask: 'Why, Daddy?'

I thought for a moment, and searched for the right words. 'If you open that door, then we will all be sucked out to a hideous death, OK?' (Subtlety has always been one of my strengths.)

Richard looked at me again, fingers still on that handle. I could see what he was thinking, 'Well, you're a big killjoy. You drag me on to this plane, the bloke in front of me is snoring like a rhino in labour, there's nothing to do, and now I can't even play with this interesting-looking door handle which is painted a funny colour. What's your problem, Dad?'

Of course he didn't say that. He said: 'Why, Daddy?'

The fact is, my son was playing with something that was potentially very dangerous, but it looked great to him. I think that exactly the same is true of sin. (I know the word 'sin' seems a bit old-fashioned, but I can't think of a better word to describe missing the mark of God's best.) Sin looks very attractive at first glance, but it is actually dangerous, deceptive and hollow.

Satan, the 'Father of lies',[33] has been working overtime on a propaganda mission that was first launched in the Garden of Eden. Way back then he managed to convince Adam and Eve that the forbidden fruit was 'good for food and pleasing to the eye, and also desirable for gaining wisdom'.[34]

This Satan is a shifty character; forget the cartoon caricature image. He doesn't have horns, has probably never carried a pitchfork in his entire life and is certainly not an effeminate-looking jester who wears a black coat and red tights.

On the contrary, the devil is a well-dressed top salesman (he loves to put his 'angel of light' gear on)[35] who could sell sand to the Arabs. Hence the Eden transaction. The true nature of sin was cleverly disguised by satanic whispers, and the catastrophe of the fall was the result.

Today the sales campaign continues. Sin still wears its ancient disguise, and thousands get taken in by the con. We find it very difficult to believe that sin is a bad deal. So a society struggling with the Aids virus refuses to change its sexual ethics. Instead, we become the 'condom culture' because sin still looks good.

That's why Jesus, as he continued the parable, painted a shocking portrait to describe the mess that the Prodigal ended up in. Some of the things that Jesus said would have stunned his Jewish listeners – particularly the Pharisees. I believe that he chose his words carefully. Jesus unmasked sin.

Look at what you're missing . . .

Christians occasionally find themselves wondering if they're missing out on the real action and fun of life.

Last week I spoke to a number of trainee Christian workers, who are giving a year of their lives to serve God. What a wonderful, lively, committed group! But I was particularly encouraged as one young man stood up and shared how he occasionally had those 'Am I missing out?' feelings. I imagine that he had probably lived a fairly party-orientated life prior to becoming a Christian. Now he no longer did some of the things that he and his friends used to do without thinking. It wasn't surprising that he sometimes wondered if life was passing him by now he was a Christian. I was glad that he was honest enough to stand up and share those feelings.

Come on, get real! We've all experienced those uncomfortable moments when we wake up during a particularly boring church meeting; the worship has been as exciting as watching paint dry, the speaker is sharing part 47 of the everlasting sermon series 'The kidneys and gall-bladders in Leviticus', and that horrible thought just won't go away: 'What if this Christian stuff is all a load of rubbish, and I'm living straight for nothing?'

Adrian Plass went through a time when 'sin looked attractive, and trying seemed more like gloom than glory'; this poem expresses his dilemma:

Who made those poison pools
In desert lands
So sweet and cool
A welcome lie
The chance to die with water on my lips
I've seen how others try to die unpoisoned in the sun
I do not think that I can do as they have done.[36]

47

So what can we learn from the Prodigal about sin? Just what *are* we missing?

The facts

Sin will cost you

> The younger son got together all he had . . . and squandered his wealth in wild living.

I'm increasingly suspicious of those special free deals that promise me something wonderful without cost. I spent five years living in America, and I remember the day when I received a letter that had an exciting message written in three-inch print on the envelope: 'Jeff Lucas has won five million dollars!'

I couldn't believe my eyes. I quickly ripped open the envelope. At that moment I actually thought that I had become a millionaire. Then I saw the small message written in tiny letters beneath the big announcement: 'If he is one of our lucky prizewinners.' Big words, the suggestion of promise, but nothing to show for it today.

Sin is often presented to us as a special free deal at no cost to us. Adam and Eve believed the sales presentation back in Eden. They got a letter from Satan, with a great promise printed on the front. 'Adam and Eve can join the Godhead today!' it declared; but then, in smaller letters underneath, it said: 'If they eat this fruit.' Satan promised them the earth, literally.

Of course, it was a confidence trick. The fact is that it is quite impossible for Satan freely to give anything good to anyone. We need to understand that, and then we won't be taken in by his schemes. In the history of the human race, Satan has *never once* given a good gift away.

For one thing, it's not in his nature to give good gifts. Jesus had the devil sized up accurately, and described him as the 'thief [who] comes only to steal and kill and destroy'.[37] Satan has the longest criminal record in cosmic history, and his speciality is fraud (he's been guilty on about 300 billion counts!). It's helpful to know who you're doing business with.

Only God the Father can give good gifts; he has the exclusive franchise in the good-gifts area. Scripture is emphatic: 'Every good and perfect gift is from above, coming down from the Father of the heavenly lights.'[38]

So in Eden, the serpent whispered his special offer.

Promise: 'You won't die if you eat.'

Reality: Not only did they die, but they brought death to the entire human race.

Promise: 'Your eyes will be opened.'

Reality: Their eyes were opened all right – to sin, shame, degradation and pain.

Promise: 'You'll be like God himself.'

Reality: Far from moving into an exalted position with God, they ended up hiding behind the bushes when God walked through the garden.

Make no mistake, this con-artist will pull the same stunt with us if we'll let him.

The price we pay? For a start, our sense of peace with God goes out of the window. Self-worth plummets to zero. When moral failure is involved, we lose the respect of our family and friends.

Over the years I have seen a number of Christian leaders 'fall' into immorality (actually no-one 'falls' . . . we jump). Playing into the hands of the thief, they lost everything: their marriages, their children, their calling, their commitment to God – and for what?

I'll be blunt: in some cases, they lost it all for the sake of a hurried orgasm in a hotel room. A high price indeed. And for those who aren't Christians, sin demands the ultimate price: an eternity spent banished from God's friendship and love.

Sometimes others get the bill. I have a colleague in the USA who, together with his family, is currently paying someone else's bill. He is a minister, and he and his wife began their married life full of bright hope, determined to serve the Lord together for all of their days. When she was pregnant with her second child, the wife had to have a blood transfusion. She was given contaminated blood. A few months later, she gave birth to a beautiful baby – with Aids. Both mum and baby have since died.

That's not fair, but then whoever said that Satan plays by the Queensberry Rules? Tragically, it's often the innocent who have to pay a heavy price for someone else's lifestyle and sin.

Sin cost the Prodigal everything – he blew his inheritance and had nothing to show for it. If you're walking with God, then take it from me: you're not missing out on anything that's either good or free.

Sin degrades

[The Prodigal] went and hired himself out to a citizen of that country, who sent him to his fields to *feed pigs*.

Jesus pulled no punches: suddenly the parable became X-rated material as far as the Pharisees in the crowd were concerned. The idea of a *Jewish* boy becoming a hired hand on a pig farm – unthinkable! The Rabbis had a saying: 'Cursed be the man who would breed swine.' This aversion to pork was more than Jewish tradition.

Scripture supported their view: 'And the pig . . . it is unclean for you.'[39]

When Jesus had the Prodigal sign on as a farm hand, he was showing the 'good' Jewish folks in the crowd just how low sin will take you. And it got worse! The boy runs out of food; with a growling stomach he begins to long for the 'pods that the pigs were eating'. The 'pods' were husks from the carob tree. Even today they are eaten by the poor, but in the Bible days they were mainly used for cattle feed. Think of it: the Prodigal had been living in the fast lane, wining and dining at the best places, and now he ends up longing to eat from a trough!

Jesus chose an image to make his point painfully clear: a Jewish pig-farm worker, surrounded by filth, with his face in the swill. No dignity left. Down and very much out.

This is what sin will do for you: it degrades. That's why pornography is a favoured weapon in hell's arsenal, for it has a double effect. Those who buy it very quickly get addicted; they start to loath themselves and feel unclean and worthless. Their dignity is progressively destroyed as they sink into further depths of perversion.

The models are emotionally raped as well, their self-worth sold to the highest bidder. The eyes of a prostitute, a drug addict, or an alcoholic tell the same story: empty, lifeless, the sparkle gone. In the end, just like the Prodigal, sin makes us feel like little more than animals. We forget that we were made in the image and likeness of God himself.[40]

The pleasure of sin is temporary

Saturday night used to be my favourite time of the week, because it was the night to get outrageously drunk. (Readers with a sensitive disposition will be pleased to know that this was before I became a Christian!) My emotions went into turbo drive when I had too much to drink. I loved everybody, and would run around the party telling everyone just how fantastic I thought they were. I would get really brave, and ask girls to dance without a second thought. (Without a few beers, I'd spend all evening trying to work up the courage to make an approach.) And I was so *happy*! Life was wonderful, I had the greatest friends, the most beautiful girlfriend (we'd be together for ever) and I was ecstatic . . . for about five hours.

Then I'd go home. For some reason, my bed wouldn't stop spinning round and round and round, and I knew what underwear felt like in a spin drier. I'd lie there with that awful feeling: 'I feel sick. I want to be sick. I'd like to be sick more than anything else in the world right now! It's not going to happen now, but sometime in the next few hours . . . I'm going to be sick.' Then a fever would set in. I would rush into the bathroom, lie flat on the floor, prostrate beside the toilet bowl and press my face against the wonderful coldness of the porcelain . . . it was awful.

Make no mistake, the enemy will take you and me as low as we are willing to go. Don't be surprised at some of the temptations that pop into your head. If the devil has the audacity to invite the Son of God to become a satanist ('Bow down and worship me', Matthew 4:9), he'll certainly try a few tricks on us.

Worst of all, the happy feeling had gone. I didn't love everybody any more. Where were my friends now? Why had that girl gone off with someone else? And then a heavy-handed drummer would start laying down a pounding backbeat on the inside of my skull. The laughs and the bright lights seemed far away as I lay there, with a cold toilet as my best friend!

The Prodigal learned the hard way that sin may be fun for a while, but the effect soon wears off. He gave himself to 'wild living'. (A more accurate translation of the word that Jesus used would be 'riotous' or 'reckless'.) Obviously you have lots of friends when the cash is freely flowing: it is quite hard to have a 'riotous time' on your own.

But then the money ran out, and the friends and the fun ran with it. Of course, the fun often runs out *before* the money.

Like a drug: the law of diminishing returns

Ask anybody who has experimented with non-prescription drugs about the law of diminishing returns. Simply put, the first time you use a drug, you need only a little to get high. It doesn't take much to send you into orbit! Then that law kicks in, and you find that you need to take more and more just to get that same high. Two tablets used to send you to Mars and back; now you need four, or five, or six.

It's like that with sin. Gradually we find that we need to get more and more daring in order just to get the same thrill. Perhaps that's why some rock stars develop bizarre habits when they stay in hotels. Normal folks like to watch television; certain music personalities prefer to rip television sets out of the hotel wall and hurl them out of previously unopened windows, an inane crusade in search of elusive fun.

We're missing nothing of value

Jesus ripped the veneer off sin, and showed us what it really will bring us: it will cost us dearly, because the tempter is a robber. It will bring a loss of dignity, because the tempter wants us to believe that we belong in the zoo (or on the farm) anyway. It will bring no lasting satisfaction, for though sin can be fun for a while, it doesn't last.

That's the truth. Will we believe it? You see, the fraud continues even as you read these words. Right now people are making moral choices that will affect the rest of their lives – and they're being conned.

Whose fool are you?

I'm convinced that the devil thinks we're stupid, and I don't like it when people insult my intelligence. Sin is actually the ultimate stupidity. Why should we be taken in by the devil? Let's wake up and see the truth, and refuse to be conned.

Paul once said, 'I have forgiven . . . in order that Satan might not outwit us. For we are not unaware of his schemes.'[41] Paul was delighted to be a 'fool' for Christ's sake,[42] but refused to be an idiot for the devil!

Whose fool are we?

54

chapter three

Repentance for real

When he came to his senses, he said, 'How many of my father's hired men have food to spare, and here I am starving to death! I will set out and go back to my father and say to him: Father, I have sinned against heaven and against you. I am no longer worthy to be called your son; make me like one of your hired men.' So he got up and went to his father.

The bucket was heavy; or was it just that he was getting weaker? He emptied the steaming swill into the trough, and immediately pandemonium broke out among the pigs. It was like this every time. There was plenty for all of them, but still they pushed and squealed and jostled each other.

How he hated the pigs, the ferocity that blazed in their eyes as they noisily gulped down as much as they could swallow!

And then the tragic irony of it all hit him as he watched them shoving and snorting, frantic to get their share. Even the pigs were better off than he was! They were filthy, disgusting . . . and fat.

He thought of home. For ages he'd worked hard at

shutting out the memories. It was too painful to remember his father's tears: tears that flowed because of him. But this time he allowed his mind to wander. Even the mere thought of home was luxurious. It seemed light, warm, inviting. Why, even the servants were well taken care of. Suddenly, almost before he knew it, the images tumbled in on him: his father's smiling face, his brother, friends, visions from the past.

The pigs were finishing their meal. All at once he knew what he must do. Quickly, without even pausing to gather the scraps of possessions he had left, he unlatched the gate of the pigpen, closed it behind him and walked away. He didn't pause to look back.

In the space of just a few short hours, the Prodigal experienced a total and complete transformation. Poverty was replaced by plenty; pig feed was dropped from his diet, because now the finest steak available was on the menu. The tears of loneliness were wiped away, and laughter came with friends and family. What was it that turned the Prodigal's night into day, and catapulted him from the pigpen back to the warmth of home? One word provides the answer: repentance. He was a long way from home, both in distance and in heart, but repentance was the bridge between sour pork and home sweet home.

Don't turn the page yet!

Mention the word 'repentance' and all kinds of images come to mind. An old man with a flat cap standing outside the railway station, holding a banner that screams, 'Repent! The end of the world is nigh.' He hands out crumpled pieces of paper that proclaim a stern gospel message, typeset in the 1930s, his face grimly consistent with his banner . . .

A fiery preacher only just manages to avoid bursting a blood vessel as he hollers the word 'repent' at his cowering congregation . . .

At the end of the service, the organist plays something suitably sombre, and the people, many of them crying, walk to the front of the church and kneel at the wooden 'altars', where paper tissues have thoughtfully been provided. Shoulders shake as they cry out to God for mercy . . .

The word 'repentance' needs some definition; it's often used without explanation. Some years ago, there was something of a fuss following a visit to Britain from the 'Kansas City prophets'. During their time here, national revival was prophesied. This announcement was greeted with scepticism by some leading evangelical figures, because, as they said, 'We all need to repent first.'

Now any student of revival will tell you that repentance has always played a key part in revivals, but what *exactly* is being called for? What does it mean to be a repentant church? What should we repent of? Is repentance synonymous with remorse? Perhaps we can answer these and other questions as we trace the Prodigal's footsteps on the road towards home.

Don't just cry

Tears are often seen as a sign of repentance, and the fact is that tears often accompany great moves of God. George Whitefield noted that, as the working classes found their way to God, 'white gutters were made on their cheeks by their tears'. Charles Finney reported that on one occasion, following an extended time of intercessory prayer, he walked into a textile factory, and just looked at the assembled workers. An amazing miracle – a preacher who said nothing! The silent sermon produced a remarkable response: the workers just burst into tears and began to cry out to God. David Brainerd laboured in prayer for the Indians with such intensity that he was coughing up blood, but the prayer paid great dividends. He walked into an Indian village, and found people crying uncontrollably. 'It was like an invisible wind was blowing, people fell under the power of God.'

Tears and sorrow often accompany revival and repentance, but we mustn't confuse sorrow with repentance itself. The logical step from that error is to believe that if we are to live in a state of repentance all the time, then we must always be crying and groaning whenever we talk to God. Amazing though it may seem, some Christians actually live that way.

I've often seen what I can only describe as 'McDonalds intercession' take place when leaders get together to pray before a church meeting. I use the 'McDonalds' name because it's a fast-food type of prayer. One of the leaders says, 'Let's commit this meeting to the Lord.' Dutifully we bow our heads, and immediately the five or six men and women, who seconds ago were quite happy, enjoying a laugh or a joke together, suddenly go into 'intercession' mode. 'Ooooooh God,' they groan, 'pleeeeease bless this meeting.' One or two make crying noises. Then, suddenly, it's over almost before it began. Someone says 'Amen', the tears disappear, and we all become happy again. Why?

Most of it is learned behaviour. We've seen someone else really getting through to God with tears and groaning, so we feel that's the way to go. But the fact is that we have often confused tears and emotional response with repentance itself.

The Bible does talk about 'godly sorrow [that] brings repentance'.[43] A more accurate translation would be 'godly grief', but however you translate it, this sorrow happens *before* repentance – it doesn't constitute repentance itself. That's why Christians are often seen praying with tears at 'altars' Sunday after Sunday, yet no real change of lifestyle results. They *are* sad about their sin, it makes them feel guilty and uncomfortable, but the sorrow they feel doesn't lead to anything of substance, so they go round in circles, from sorrow to sin to sorrow to sin.

'Shall we give it a go?'

I used to believe that a really good conversion experience should be fairly emotional – the wetter the better! Then I met Gary and Jan. They came into an evangelistic meeting as a result of a leaflet being put through their door.

When the speaker concluded, he invited people to respond to the gospel. Gary and Jan put their hands up to declare their interest, and afterwards squeezed themselves into the room that had been set aside for counselling. I sat down with them, and began to go over the gospel story. I talked about sin, death and the cross. They listened with interest, but showed no apparent emotion; I wondered what they were thinking.

At last it was time for me to put the $64,000 question:

'Now then, Gary and Jan, you've heard what the speaker said. I've explained the message and answered your questions. Now it's up to you. Do you want to make Jesus Christ your Lord right now?'

Gary wasn't crying. He didn't grab hold of my ankles and scream, 'Yes, yes, I need to be saved, now!' He turned to Jan, and said: 'What do you think, love? Shall we give it a go?'

I was stunned. What kind of response was that?

Jan smiled and nodded. ('Wonderful!' I thought. 'She wants to give it a go.')

Gary also expressed his desire to 'give the King of kings a bit of a try', so, without much faith, I led them in a prayer, and, thrusting a booklet at them, I shook them by the hand and thought I'd never see them again. It was hardly a 'textbook' conversion.

Gary and Jan, however, became 'textbook' Christians! Almost from the start they were committed, eager to learn, and ultimately became fine local church leaders. Today they are as keen for God as ever. So don't judge a conversion by the tears – or lack of them!

Repentance: a return to reality

When [the Prodigal] came to his senses, he said . . .

The first step of the long walk home was taken when the boy woke up in the pigpen. Things were so dark, so desperate, that the truth finally dawned: 'This is madness. I want to go home.' I like the way one translator puts it: 'When he came to himself.' Like a man who suddenly sees himself reflected in a mirror, and so 'comes to himself' as he steps nearer to take a closer look, so the boy finally realized that he had spent his time running from everybody, including himself. Sin has a sedating effect: it blurs our sense of focus so much that we no longer see what and who we really are. But for the Prodigal the pigpen became a place of reality. Stirring himself from a moral coma, the younger son brought his dreaming to an end and started to deal in hard facts.

Repentance is impossible unless we are ready to face up to the reality of ourselves. If we can't see where we are, we won't be able to see where we want to go! That's why John the Baptist welcomed his congregation by saying, 'Good evening, vipers, who warned you lot to flee from the coming wrath?'

Jesus kicked tables over in church and used terms like 'blind guides', 'fools' and 'white-washed sepulchres'. Were John and Jesus into rudeness for the sake of it? Of course not. The words they used were designed to stir people out of their sleep and bring them back to reality.

That's why we must refuse to be moulded by a world addicted to activity, sit down once in a while, and allow the Lord to show us what we really are.

A breakfast of reality

Peter learned a major lesson about reality: when he first met Jesus, he was a man who had never really met himself. That's why he blurted out, 'Lord, I am ready to go with you to prison and to death.'[44]

Don't be too hard on the guy. I believe he sincerely meant what he said. While Peter was rather good at operating with his brain in neutral and his mouth in fifth gear, this was more than just big talk; he probably really believed that he would be able to follow through with loyalty even to the death.

But the Peter we find after he denied Christ with curses is a different man altogether. On one occasion, Jesus arrives in his post-resurrection body to cook his friends some breakfast and dish up some reality to Peter. Check out the story in John 21. The disciples are sitting round a charcoal fire, and Jesus is cooking some fish. There's total silence as the chef does his work: they watch his nail-scarred hands, adjusting the fish over the flames.

Think about it! It was while he was sitting by a charcoal fire that Peter denied Jesus with curses.[45] Now, quietly, Peter remembers, and breakfast began with reality for first course.

After breakfast, Jesus asks Peter: 'Do you love me?' The word Jesus used (which we translate 'love') is the word *agapeō*. This is the highest form of deep, constant love. What will Peter say? Will he deliver another self-deluded little speech about how he loves Jesus more than anybody else?

No, Peter has faced some reality. He replies, 'Yes, Lord, you know that I love you.' On the surface this seems like a simple answer, except that Peter drops the word *agapeō* when replying and instead says, 'You know that I love [*phileō*] you.' *Philia* is a lesser love than *agapē*, a 'tender affection'.[46]

Preachers have condemned Peter for refusing to affirm *agapē* love for Jesus, instead professing *philia*. I commend him. At long last, he's facing up to reality about himself. Real repentance is going on here.

Repentance: stop passing the buck

'I will set out and go back to my father . . .'

Reality showed the Prodigal what a mess he was in, and that he alone was responsible for that mess. No-one else was to blame.

What a contrast to the attitude which so appears to pervade today! Sometimes it seems that the last person we should blame for crime is the criminal!

'It's his past.'

'It's his upbringing.'

'It's his schooling.'

'It's the environment.'

Passing the buck has become such a science that some victims of rape have been made to feel more criminal than their assailants: 'Well, she was out alone after dark. She was asking for it, wasn't she?'

When President Kennedy was shot, some newspapers suggested that it was the socio-economic situation of Dallas, Texas, that was to blame, rather than Lee Harvey Oswald.

Anna Russell laments the demise of personal responsibility:

> I went to my psychiatrist to be psychoanalysed,
> To find out why I killed the cat and blacked my
> husband's eyes.
> He laid me on a downy couch to see what he could
> find,
> And here is what he dredged up from my
> subconscious mind . . .

When I was five my mummy hid my dolly in a trunk,
And so it follows naturally that I am always drunk.
When I was six I saw my father kiss the maid one
    day,
And that is why I suffer from kleptomania.

When I was eight I suffered from ambivalence to
    my brothers
And that is why, now, I poison all my lovers.
But I am happy, for I've learned the lesson this has
    taught:
That everything I do that's wrong is someone else's
    fault.[47]

Don't blame me: I've got a pet demon

I welcome the fact that the church is beginning to engage in spiritual warfare, both at a personal deliverance level, and through prayer walking, March for Jesus and the like. Praise God for these initiatives! Ignoring the devil won't make him go away!

In knowing that, we must be careful not to emphasize deliverance so much that we neglect teaching about personal growth and development. Some years ago the church in Britain went through one of its hyper-deliverance phases. We armed ourselves with our safari guns and went demon-hunting. At that time, it seemed that demons were in no danger of being an endangered species – there were millions of them, or so it seemed.

Every sin imaginable had a demon named in its honour. Some demons were named after some very wholesome things, like laughter, for example. I can remember a deliverance session that was held while I was at Bible college. A couple of hunters had gathered around an unfortunate student. The exorcists had two major beliefs about spiritual warfare: (1) the devil is deaf (hence the need to scream and shout at the top of your voice); (2) demons are shy about personal introduction ('*Name yourself!*' was the most frequently hollered command).

The alleged demoniac obviously found the ranting and raving to be rather amusing, so he started to chuckle. Triumphantly, the hunters realized that they had made a major breakthrough: '*Come out, you foul spirit of laughter!*' they yelled.

While it's obviously true that demonic forces can exploit us when we allow sin to rule in our lives, there is a danger that we can blame our character flaws on demons. It's actually a very attractive idea: first, because we don't have to take the blame ('The devil made me do it') and furthermore no effort or will is required from us ('One of these days I'll get delivered'). In a 'Nescafé' society that loves quick fixes and instant answers, it's easy to blame anybody, or anything, for that which is actually our fault. As Scripture says, 'Each of us will give an account of himself to God.'[48] Repentance is well on the way when we face facts and say, 'The buck stops here.' If we refuse to take responsibility for ourselves and to make choices and changes, then we will end up going nowhere fast.

Pat Hurley says, 'Maturity is measured by the length of time it takes us to deal with personal sin.' Don't procrastinate about taking responsibility. Zacchaeus did what was right the moment he *understood* what was right. During lunch with Jesus he said, 'Look, Lord! Here and now I give half of my possessions to the poor.'[49]

Repentance: giving the pigs
a permanent wave

Imagine it. 'Dad, I'm so glad to see you. Thanks for welcoming me home. There's just one thing: I thought I'd bring the pigs with me; we got really close, you see. They even shared their food with me. Oh yes, we had many a happy evening supping swill together. It'll be all right – they can stay in my room.'

Yes, I know it's an absurd thought. The Prodigal had to say farewell to the pigs for good before going home. Repentance means that we leave behind (or lay aside, to use a more biblical turn of phrase) those things that are going to be a snare for our future with God.

Leaving on a jet plane

I was late for the plane, my bag weighed a ton; I ran as fast as I could through New York airport, desperate to get to the gate in time. Ahead of me was just one obstacle: security. Every passenger has to walk through an archway that contains a metal detector; if you are carrying a tactical nuclear warhead, or anything metal for that matter, a buzzer will sound, and you'll have to leave the missile behind if you want to get on the plane.

I put my bag on the X-ray machine, and then I saw her. She was the meanest-looking security lady I have ever seen. She had tatoos on her tatoos. Her face was fixed in a 'go ahead, make my day' look. My heart was filled with fear, because I knew that this woman could break my arms with a mere flick of an eyelash. I walked through the archway.

It happened. The bell rang.

The woman leapt up, and rushed across to me. She

was angry – or was that just a hint of a malicious smile in her eyes?

What had made the bell ring? I searched quickly through my pockets, and discovered the culprit: a travel alarm clock (the type favoured by terrorists, who strap those clocks to bombs).

The Wild Woman of Wongamonga was angry. 'What's this?' she hissed.

I thought, 'Bless her heart. She's not over-endowed in the old brains department.' But I said, 'It's an alarm clock, my sweet.'

With a half-squeal not unlike that of a dying animal, she asked, 'What's it for?'

I told her the truth: 'It wakes you up in the morning.'

She insisted that I lay the offending timepiece aside, and invited me to go through the arch again. I did, and this time there was no buzzer. Bliss! The sun came out, the lady smiled a toothless smile, and the birds began to sing again.

But I had to lay aside that clock. The alternative? I'd not only miss my flight, I'd go nowhere. I'd be stuck at the gate; arguing, frustrated, but stuck all the same.

Don't get me wrong: God is no cosmic security guard (and actually the dear lady was simply doing her job). He is a loving Father, and wants the very best for us. That's why we stand still when we refuse to lay down what will ultimately only hurt God, us and those around us. God likes us too much to let us get away with it.

Repentance: back home to Dad

Obviously, there were mixed motives in the Prodigal's heart. A growling stomach brought an amazing clarity to his thinking! Notwithstanding that, his decision was to return to his father; not the warmth of his bed, or the plenty of his father's kitchen, but to Dad himself.

The heart of repentance is the restoration of our friendship with God, not just a return to a morality or ethic. That relationship must be the driving force behind our thirst for integrity. As Paul puts it, 'The love of Christ constrains us.'

It's amazing what you'll do when you're in love. You laugh at each other's hopelessly unfunny jokes, and exchange kisses first thing in the morning when you look more like a haystack than a human being. Why? Is it just because you made a vow, so it's in the contract? No, love is the driving force, not law.

Sadly, some Christians treat repentance as an insurance premium payment. 'I'd better get right with God, because Jesus might come soon!'

I wish we'd all been ready

In early 1988, *66 Reasons for the Rapture* was published in the USA. It created a sensation among Christians, selling millions of copies. The thesis of the book was that the rapture would take place on one of three days in September 1988. The author, a retired NASA scientist, claimed to have spent his whole life researching Bible chronology and now he was convinced that he had got the figure-work right. On a radio interview, he said apparently, 'If Jesus doesn't come in September 1988, then the Bible is wrong!'

Amazingly, millions of Christians bought into the idea. People had their pets put down, because they didn't want them left behind after the vertical take-off! Others ran up huge credit-card bills (Jesus would come before the bill arrived – very responsible. I call it 'escapology eschatology').

But something more disturbing happened. Thousands of previously backslidden Christians got right with God and began to join the church. It was said (but never corroborated) that around 100,000 people became Christians in early September.

Of course Jesus didn't come! Undeterred, the author issued yet another book, saying that he'd got the date wrong by exactly one year . . .

While God clearly exhorts us to be ready at all times for the return of Christ, be it in a 'rapture' or whatever, the primary basis of repentance is a return to the warmth of Father's arms. Nobody can stay motivated by a series of cold religious principles for very long. Repentance brings us back to Father, not just to evangelical orthodoxy.

Repentance: 'Bless me, Father, for I have sinned'

'Father, I have sinned against heaven and against you.'

The first words the Prodigal uttered on his return were words of openness and truth. There's no attempt to hedge the issue or cover up; no 'mitigating circumstances to be taken into consideration'. He just blurts it out and stands there, defenceless, at his dad's mercy. 'I've sinned.'

He confesses the *extent* of his sin as well. His was a sin against God *and* man, so he uses the phrase, 'Against heaven, and against you.' A lot of people have been hurt – now the confession is refreshingly forthright.

While most of us don't need to be reminded about confession to God, we have tended to play down confessing to one another. Evangelicalism has reacted against Roman Catholic *ecclesiastical* confession, where the sinner goes to the priest and is offered absolution. We have rightly declared that 'there is one God and one mediator between God and men, the man Christ Jesus',[50] but I believe we have over-reacted.

Priestly confession isn't required, because we are all priests before God (even though many of us still hold to an unbiblical distinction between clergy and laity, which is about 2,000 years out of date). But what about *relational* confession, where we openly share our faults and struggles and hold ourselves accountable to one another? We have made sin a private matter, 'just between me and Jesus'. The Scriptures take a different view: 'Therefore confess your sins to each other and pray for each other so that you may be healed.'[51]

Pretending in the church: the epidemic

Best-selling author Gordon MacDonald is one of the few major figures who has made a full recovery from moral failure. After writing *Ordering Your Private World*, his personal world collapsed. We should all be thankful that MacDonald humbly submitted himself to the discipline of his church, stepped aside from ministry, and allowed his life to be rebuilt. His life is now a glowing example of the redemptive power of God: with Jesus, there's always another chance.

During that twilight period of adultery, MacDonald found himself living a lie, and he made a statement that we all need to hear: 'Pretending is the common cold of the church.' Far from being a people who are really honest about ourselves, we hide behind a veneer of respectability. We shy away from relationships of any depth, preferring 'close encounters of an evangelical kind' in the church foyer every Sunday.

Pretence was one of the first skills that I developed as a young Christian. It was no-one's fault but my own, but I became a master at it.

You see, church came as quite a shock to me. I'd only really ever been exposed to the 'God slot' syndrome on the TV, where large groups of people stand around looking like they have just had their feet collectively run over by a rather large truck. And then I met Christians who smiled a lot. Even during the service! I found these apparently bionic grinaholics quite disturbing. It seemed as if they had absolutely no problems at all. The only struggles I heard about were in the past tense.

I remember the first night of Bible college. It was testimony time. A guy stood up and thrilled us for about twenty minutes with details of his scintillating life of sin (he used to go out and get drunk every Saturday night with his grandmother, which I thought was rather novel, and the dear lady would get so legless that he had to wheel her home in a wheelbarrow). A rich and lurid tapestry of dubious activity was spread before us, after which, in the final twenty seconds, he announced, 'And then I gave my life to Jesus,' and sat down. Apparently there were no more problems after conversion, but apparently not much of anything else either!

We used to sing songs like 'I am H-A-P-P-Y'. This great classic was full of doctrinal meat:

I am h-a-p-p-y,
I am h-a-p-p-y.

71

> I know I am, I'm sure I am,
> I am h-a-p-p-y.

Another weighty rendition was:

> It isn't any trouble just to s-m-i-l-e.
> It isn't any trouble just to s-m-i-l-e.
> If you pack up all your troubles,
> Then they'll vanish like a bubble
> If you only take the trouble
> Just to s-m-i-l-e.

There was only one problem. I did love Jesus, but I didn't always feel like smiling, and grinning didn't make all the difficulties go away. So I was faced with a choice: do I yell 'help!' . . . or do I pretend? Shall I ask people to pray for me as I struggle with my addiction to nicotine (I'm not picking on smoking, but it was something that I was privately wanting to get rid of at that time, without too much success) . . . or do I buy thirty-one packets of Trebor mints before every church meeting, and stick them in my mouth, ears and down my throat, so as to disguise the fact?

I decided to take the pathway of least resistance: to pretend. In fact, I was practised at the art of giving the right impression. I went out and bought the largest Bible in the history of the church, and it seemed to be surgically attached to my left armpit. Wherever I went, my Bible went. It was the in thing back then to wear a wooden cross round your neck and sport a Christian badge. I kitted myself out with the uniform: large cross (I looked like Mother Teresa in Levis) and a huge badge on my right lapel that declared in huge letters: 'Hello!

You're going to hell' or something similar.

But something was missing. I looked right, but I didn't sound right. I noticed that my friends at church would frequently use phrases like 'Praise the Lord', and 'Hallelujah', but somehow it didn't sound right coming from me. I'm embarrassed to confess that I locked myself in my bedroom, stood in front of the mirror, and practised my pious expression technique. I paid attention to every detail. Tilting my head slightly to the left, with a 'hang on, I've got a blessing coming on' look in my eyes, I went over the words repeatedly until I thought I'd got it just right: 'Praaaise the Lord!'

What a fearful way to live – terrified lest you should be discovered for what you really are. This is a million miles from the kingdom! The place where God rules is a place of light and truth, where we're set free from the need to prove that we're something we're not!

Repentance with a yell

The ministry of John the Baptist is a good example of the importance of confession as part of repentance. Those being baptized by him in the Jordan confessed their sins, apparently just before going under the water.[52] The Greek word for 'confess' (*exomologeō* for anyone who's interested) means 'to confess forth, freely, openly, a public acknowledgment of sins'. Imagine that! This was so much more than a nice little religious ceremony. As John 'prepared the way of the Lord', he introduced people to reality and openness at a deeply personal level.

The same thing happened in Ephesus during a major revival among a group of occultists.[53] A huge bonfire was built, and the equivalent of 2.5 million poundsworth of occult material was burned, and the people 'openly confessed their evil deeds'.

Do you see the connection? As the people got serious about God, they got seriously real about themselves. By the way, it's that word *exomologeō* again.

And *exomologeō* pops up in James's instructions about prayer for the sick. He talks about the God who hears us pray when we are in trouble; enjoys our worship when we praise, and will heal as we take authority in his name. Then, right in the middle of all that, he says, 'Confess your sins (*exomologeō* again) to each other.'

It's great to have people around you who know you rather well and still love you. There's tremendous safety and freedom in being known.

Don't hang out your laundry in the foyer

The revival situations mentioned in John's ministry and at Ephesus are examples of public repentance, which may well happen in a situation where lots of people are coming to faith at once.

In our ongoing life together as a church, it's more likely that confession should be taking place within the context of trusted friendships which have been steadily built, and in situations of accountability to leaders. Next time someone whom you vaguely know asks, 'How are you?' in the church foyer, resist the temptation to give them a copy of your medical report, including a documented list of every sin committed in the last twenty-five years.

Gerald Coates often talks about three stages of friendship. *Veneer* is when Christians are so nice, 'they are nicer than God himself'.[54] *Disillusionment* is the second, where we face up to the reality of humanity in

74

the church. Think of it like this: everybody in the church is probably just like you and me. In one sense the church is something of a hospital where broken people are being put together, so don't be surprised if you see some blood and broken bones around. If you find a perfect church, don't join it – you'll ruin it.

The third stage is *opt out or choose reality*. This is that rugged stage where you commit yourself to friendship without naïvety, or you opt out and charge backwards to superficiality again.

Durable kingdom relationships, where openness and truth flow easily, don't just happen. They are built. It's risky, but believe me, it's worth it!

Openness doesn't mean being stubborn

One last word about confession as an element of repentance: please notice that this is confession *with a purpose*. I've occasionally met folk who are more than happy to be honest about themselves, but less happy actually to engage their will and commit themselves to change. The attitude is, 'This is me, pal. I'm obnoxious, arrogant, unteachable and immoral. I'm willing to be upfront about my stinking self, but if you don't like it, tough, because you have to accept me as I am.'

The Prodigal was honest about himself because he wanted to change. Confession is a redemptive principle. That's why James says, 'Confess your sins to each other . . . and pray for each other that you may be healed.' The confession is valid only in that it is the first step along a pathway of transformation through prayer and the power of the Holy Spirit.

'To be honest, brother . . . I hate you'

Some folk use reality and confession as an opportunity to be extremely rude in Jesus' name.

As one who speaks publicly in churches a lot, I am gathering an extensive collection of after-church insults. I know that I'm in trouble when the person comes up and says, 'What I'm going to say is in love, brother.' Time to put the tin helmet on.

One guy came up and said, 'When you stood up today, I hated you. God has convicted me. I must be honest, of course, and I need to confess this to you!'

Thanks a lot! You didn't need to confess anything. You needed to get your attitude right between you and God. Rather than confession, that's dumping garbage in the name of God.

A lady wandered up and said, 'I hope you don't mind me asking, but have you ever had a stroke?'

'Why do you ask?' I queried.

'Because when you smile, only one side of your face goes up.'

I had to laugh. I was tempted to say, 'No, I'm just seriously ugly. What's your excuse?'

Openness is about honesty that prepares us for the power to change. It's about living in a harness of accountability that is actually very liberating. It's a million miles from, 'I know I'm a stinker, but I'm never going to change, so just love me anyway.' Rudeness with a tinge of sanctification is out of order.

Repentance: restitution may be appropriate

'Make me like one of your hired servants.'

The inheritance had been squandered, a considerable amount of money down the drain. So as the Prodigal returns, he leaves behind his 'I want my rights; give me what's mine' attitude. That was for the pigpen. In its place is a willingness to serve and make restitution, so he offers his services for an unlimited time, to work off his debt.

As in the case of Zacchaeus, the Prodigal's attitude of repentance travelled from his heart to his wallet – a sure sign that something genuine had taken place.

Restitution may not always be possible: there are some things beyond our control. As a youngster, I did a lot of petty stealing from a local sweetshop. The shop has since closed (hopefully the demise of the business wasn't caused by my filling my pockets with gobstoppers). The owners have moved away. There's nothing I can do. There *are* times, however, when the Holy Spirit makes it clear that restitution can and should be made. It can be costly.

John: crooked policeman gone straight

John (not his real name) was a policeman with the London Metropolitan Force. Most Saturdays he was on duty patrolling football matches, working on crowd control and surveillance.

John's bosses began to pressurize for results, and, for the police, arrests and convictions are results. Hooliganism was becoming an increasing problem and the people in authority wanted to be able to show that they were making an impact. During one game, a fan attracted John's attention; the man had a reputation as a real troublemaker. It was time for an arrest. John slipped alongside the fan, planted a knife in his pocket, and arrested him. The fan was convicted on John's false evidence, and sent to prison for eighteen months. The bosses were pleased, and became braver in their thirst for results. John became part of a conspiracy to falsify evidence against a London gang. Corruption was in full swing . . . then John became a Christian.

Now he had a new perspective and a new faith, and he was aware that at least one man was behind bars because of his perjury. He went to see the leaders of his church, and, amazingly, was told to do nothing on the basis that bad publicity would result: 'You should take care of your family.'

But try as he might, he couldn't leave it there. An innocent man was in prison, and all because of him.

He went to his superiors in the police, and told them that he was going to confess his involvement in both cases. They went into orbit! Life became very difficult, and finally John spoke out.

The football fan was released. John was thrown out of the police, then arrested and sentenced to two years' imprisonment. It was far from easy in prison. He got pressure from all sides. As an ex-policeman, he was despised by the other prisoners, and as a policeman who had blown his bosses' cover, he was despised by the prison officials.

But restitution was made. John served eighteen months, and was appointed to an excellent management position almost immediately after his release (the employer knew the full details of John's history). Today, he and his family are going on with God. Restitution, in that particular situation, had to be made.

Don't panic!

Don't go rushing off to the filing cabinet of your past and start frantically thumbing through past sins to find out where you need to make restitution. Sometimes it's impossible, or unnecessary. The Prodigal offered to work off his debt, and Dad didn't take him up on the offer. Please don't get bound up in the idea that *every* sin against others needs to be worked through in restitution. What we need is an open heart to the Holy Spirit, so that he can show us what, if anything, needs to be done.

The Prodigal took one step, 'having come to himself' – a step of repentance. It literally made all the difference.

II

THE FATHER

chapter four

'Meet Dad'

But while he was still a long way off, his father saw him and
was filled with compassion for him; he ran to his son.

Of course, it was probably a total waste of time, and the
rest of the family thought he was foolish, but he'd do it
anyway. The sun was slowly setting as he eased into his
chair by the window. There it was: the horizon that he'd
studied ten thousand times, but so far he'd never found
what he wanted so desperately to see. He knew every
tree, every inch of the terrain.

'Eyes aren't what they used to be,' he thought, using
his hand to deflect the glare of the retreating sun.
Suddenly, he sat bolt upright as he saw the man. He
didn't dare allow himself to be too hopeful; many times
his heart had leapt when he saw a figure in the distance,
only to be bitterly disappointed.

'He's coming this way!' Every second brought him
more into focus. Was it just the neighbour's boy? No!
The figure that had filled his thoughts every day . . . it
was him! He jumped up, threw age and caution to the
wind, and began to run.

'What you think about God determines how you live.'[55] So says Nick Cuthbert, and how right he is. A. W. Tozer takes a step further: 'What first comes into our minds when we think of God is the most important thing about us.'

Over the years I've noticed that a Christian's behaviour is mainly influenced by his overall concept of God (rather than by a collection of scriptural principles alone), and that very often people end up being 'conformed to the image' of God *as they see him*. So those with a negative view of God as the cosmic killjoy become down-beat, colourless people who don't find too much joy in life and get nervous around people who do.

Let me list a number of common misconceptions about the nature and personality of God.

God the cosmic skinhead

Ants. We used to have a major problem with them in our house. Every summer millions of them would come and camp out around the kitchen step. My mum used to put 'Nuke-ant' powder down, but I think the ants had developed a resistance to it. In fact, I think they enjoyed the stuff. You could almost hear them saying grace when she got the packet out.

So I decided to take the initiative, and deal with the problem my own way. My dad had a rather large hammer in his tool case. I sat on the back step, and waited, hammer in hand. I knew that sooner or later they would arrive. They did. An ant would appear. 'Good morning, ant,' I would venture. 'Would you like to go to heaven?'

Insect lovers and watchers of Channel 4 documentaries will be intrigued to note that no ant ever responded to that question. So, assuming from the silence that he or she did indeed want to be ushered forth to that great anthill in the sky, I would whack it with the hammer. Please don't write to me telling me how cruel I was. I don't do this sort of thing any more!

Splat! Goodbye, ant.

When I first became a Christian, I got the impression that God was like that, sitting in heaven just waiting to 'break' me with a cosmic mallet.

I had this impression that God loved me in some cold, ethereal way, but that he didn't actually *like* me. In fact, not only was God something of a threatening skinhead, but had a slightly sadistic streak in him as well. In my mind, there was no greater joy for God than to dream up something for me to do that he knew I would just hate doing!

'Don't say you don't want to be a missionary to Burma,' hollered another impassioned preacher, 'because if he hears you say that, he's going to make you go to Burma!' You'd be amazed how many Christians have admitted to me that they have heard those exact words spoken.

Think about it. God is seated in heaven, and an angel floats in and tells him that you don't like hot weather or snakes, and would definitely not like a missionary calling. A glimmer appears in God's eye: 'Wonderful! Bring out the hammer!'

This 'anything I want to do can't possibly be what God wants' theology seriously affected me when I was considering marriage. I was very concerned about marrying Kay – because I loved her and found her really attractive, and because she was everything that I desired in a wife. The idea that God might approve seemed too good to be true. At that point in my life it would have actually been much easier for me to marry someone whom I found unlovable and unattractive, because I'd be doing it for Jesus! Even as I write this it seems incredibly warped, but I can remember the nightmare that comes when you believe that the will of God is negative, ugly and automatically the opposite of any desires that you might have.

God the sober fanatic

The next logical step from a 'skinhead' theology is an intensity that is nervous of laughter. The idea is that God is a wide-eyed fanatic who is so busy working out the world's problems that he doesn't have time to see the funny side of life, so if we're being conformed to his image, then neither should we. Relaxation and hilarity are off the menu, because 'we must always be about our Father's business'. While I realize that it was Jesus who made the 'Father's business' comment, I don't think that in any way suggests that we shouldn't find time to smile, play, do things of no apparent eternal significance, and let our hair down!

I heard of a situation that took place in a Bible college one Saturday afternoon. There were no lectures, and the students decided to have a playful fight. There was no malice or damage, just a chance to let off some steam and have some fun. That is, until one of the prefects (who happened to be a rather intensely religious person) popped his head around the door and asked, 'Excuse me. Don't you know where you are?'

The students were well aware of where they were; the

wrestling hadn't caused them to lose a sense of geographical location. They told him that they knew their address, map reference, *etc.*

'No, no, no, no, no,' said the prefect (religious people like this often say 'no' five times). 'I mean, don't you know where you are?' And then it all became clear. Because they were in training for Christian ministry, the implication was that fun and a little harmless frivolity were *not* to be on the agenda. Instead of wrestling, they should have been out on the street handing out tracts!

I'm ashamed to admit that I went through the 'laughter is for the lukewarm' syndrome. In fact, I vividly recall getting on my knees one day and saying, 'God, I'm feeling happy. I must have sinned. Forgive me.'

God the blind, dumb old man with a remarkable hearing-aid (and a red coat)

The other extreme view of God is a concept of a sentimental old grandfather who is basically a total pushover. He's blind (so he doesn't see our sin), he's dumb (so he doesn't say anything of consequence, even in Scripture) but he has an amazing hearing-aid that enables him to hear all our requests for our wants and needs. Like a chocolate machine on a railway platform, he's always there to give me just what I order, as long as I use the right formula. This 'good ol' boy' God will never ask me to do anything that will involve effort, pain or sacrifice. He lives only to facilitate my personal happiness: that's why he wears a red blazer. Like a worker at a holiday camp, he just loves to cry to his people, 'Is everybody happy?' and the church calls back, 'You bet your life we are.'

Our Father

It goes without saying that all three of the above models of God are nothing short of perverse. Unfortunately, however, my experience has shown me that many evangelicals have lingering snapshots in their hearts of a skinhead, fanatic or redcoat.

An orthodox theology of the fatherhood of God is insufficient. What is needed by every one of us is a heartfelt revelation of fatherhood, for that revelation is the foundation of the Christian experience. The alphabet of Christianity begins with F for Father.

That fact is borne out in the teaching that Jesus gave his disciples on prayer. When they said, 'Lord teach us to pray!'[56] they were asking a broad question: 'How should we approach God, relate to him, and develop an ongoing friendship?'

So Jesus told them how to begin: 'Our *Father*.' He was showing us that recognition of fatherhood is the place to start. Without such a foundation, our relationship with God will be a mutation.

Will the real God please stand up?

When he described the Prodigal, Jesus effectively said, 'This is humankind – take a long look.'

Now, as the dad rushes towards the boy, Jesus says, 'Now look at God.' He is the Father who eagerly welcomes us. Remember those Pharisees who were standing at the back of the crowd when Jesus told this parable? Perhaps they were expecting Jesus to describe how the father would rebuke the boy for his law-breaking, and drive him off the farm – a picture of rebuke and punishment. 'Here comes the judge.'

They got a big shock! Jesus says that the father 'saw the boy when he was a long way off'. Why? Because he's been watching and waiting. And when he finally realizes that his son is coming back, he abandons all sense of elderly decorum (which was strong in the culture of the day) and charges across the fields to embrace him.

It's obvious that Jesus was keen for the crowd (and particularly the Pharisees) to understand this aspect of the Father God. He himself had been in trouble for welcoming sinners and eating with them;[57] that's what led him to teach this parable in the first place. Jesus was modelling an important facet of Father's personality, by making people feel special and significant. The word that the Pharisees used to describe the 'welcome' that Jesus gave literally means 'to receive someone to oneself with favour'.[58] Each and every individual was made to feel particularly welcome when Jesus was around.

So Jesus models this in lifestyle, then reinforces the principle by having the father in the story rush off to see his boy. While longsuffering is an element of God's heart towards us, he doesn't merely tolerate us. We don't come as any surprise to him. He knew what he was taking on. The boy receives a welcome while still in his filth! He doesn't stay filthy and stinking for too long, but as he was he was received. Unfortunately some Christians take that on board as far as the start of their Christian lives are concerned ('Just as I am without one plea, O Lamb of God, I come'), but then spend the rest of their lives trying to earn God's acceptance, as if God accepts sinners only the first time he meets them and thereafter becomes massively intolerant.

This picture of the welcoming, sprinting God would have created a massive stir among the Pharisees. They had an abstract, transcendental view of God. They saw God as the One who would be the 'Creator in the beginning, the Judge at the end, but in the meantime he is the far-off ruler in the universe'.[59] Even the name of God was not to be mentioned.

So when Jesus started to talk about God as Father, this in itself would have been considered radical by the Pharisees. The idea of God as Father had been fore-shadowed in the Old Testament,[60] and in other Jewish literature,[61] but it was Jesus who really brought the whole concept into sharp focus.

However, when Jesus portrayed Father as 'seeing and running', he detonated a theological atom bomb. One writer says of Jesus: 'He broke through, at the most decisive point, the transcendental ascetic spirit of Judaism.'[62]

God becomes far more than a principle of law or the basis of an ethical system. He becomes the warm-hearted lover of men, women and children everywhere. As evangelicals, we need to be careful lest we present the gospel rather than the God of the gospel. The present emphasis on signs and wonders and the prophetic will help us here. God is seen to be active and working among his people, rather than as the distant Redeemer presented in the 'Four Spiritual Laws'.

He is the Father who sees and runs. Right at this moment, Christian, God likes you and is tremendously glad that you're in his kingdom! This is vital news. We've got to grow *from* acceptance, rather than towards it.

Love that runs *and* cries: compassion

Having delivered a message guaranteed to have the Pharisees gasping on the floor and praying for an oxygen tent, Jesus takes a step further in overturning their concept of God. He describes the Father as 'filled with compassion'. The God of the Pharisees had little time for compassion, and they were like him. The law was all that mattered; they had no mercy or care for the man with the withered hand, the hungry disciples, the sick or the demonized. That's why Jesus got a red card when he healed on the Sabbath. Never mind the fact that sickness and suffering had been relieved – only principles mattered.

Again, in his own life and ministry, Jesus had modelled the Father's compassion: tears flowed when he saw the crowds 'helpless, like sheep without a shepherd'.[63] Pain and suffering moved him as well. The death of Lazarus stirred him to compassion,[64] as did the funeral of the widow of Nain's son.[65]

Now he shows the father who weeps tears of sadness and joy, face streaked as he rushes to his returning child. The word 'compassion' denotes far more than sympathy; this was a deep-seated inner yearning, an eruption of emotion in response to need and suffering.

God's love for us is no cold, passionless constant that never flares or races. Like a Victorian papa who lines his children up once a week, and routinely informs them that he loves them, but never hugs or kisses them throughout their entire lives, God's love is sometimes reduced to being something bland and benevolently boring; something there, but never quite warmly expressed or felt.

On the contrary, God gets so excited about us that sometimes he dances,[66] and so sad that he sometimes weeps.[67] This is our God!

And this is the God whom we must share with others. A church that has only an agenda to share and no heart of compassion to share it will never make an impact. Thousands of babies are aborted daily, sacrificed on the new altar of convenience. This violates God's principles, and breaks his heart. More than the thundering sheriff, he is the heartbroken dad.

The Father of encouragement: well done!

Ever been around when a child brings his first painting home from school? The family gathers round to examine the masterpiece. Dad notices that the painting appears to be a portrait of a human being, albeit a strange-looking human being. He has four legs, a head five times the normal size, and hands big enough to lift a piano with a little finger! Overall, this human being looks like he has just kissed a truck travelling at eighty miles per hour.

'Who *is* this?' asks Dad.

'It's you,' replies the proud budding Picasso.

What does Dad do? Get angry and insulted? Send the child to bed with no supper, and consign the painting to the dustbin? Such a father would need to seek psychiatric help!

The God of this parable sees, runs, feels and *kisses*. This is no English homecoming: 'Hello, old bean. I've been waiting for you, and I'm jolly glad to see you' (followed by handshake).

The Prodigal has been practising his 'I'm no good, I'm

sorry, can you give me a job?' speech over and over again until it's word perfect, but his speech is cut short as he is literally bowled over by his hugging, kissing father, and the speech disappears into his dad's armpit!

By the way, the kiss that Jesus talked about was more than a polite peck on the cheek. One writer[68] says that the word Jesus used means 'to kiss fervently'.

By now the Pharisees are having a cow! Kissing this wretch who had been made unclean by his contact with pigs? Cardiac arrests in that part of the crowd were probably imminent. But what an encouraging gesture! Hugs and kisses were reserved for sons, not slaves.

Sometimes we feel as though our service for God is a bit like that child's painting. God is the one who gives 'endurance and encouragement'.[69] Not only is that his nature, but he knows that the way to strengthen us is to encourage us. Look up the word 'encourage' in the New Testament, and you'll see that wherever it appears, the word 'strength' isn't far away. Encouragement and strength are married. The kiss of God can come to us through the word of prophecy that lifts our hearts when we're wondering if it's all worth while; by that unexpected sense of his being around when you weren't really looking for him; by that token of love that comes in the form of a friendship that enables you to laugh. Of course at the end of it all, there's a kiss of encouragement waiting for those who have served God: 'Well done, good and faithful servant.'[70]

Sometimes that kiss comes through discipline and chastening. When we as fathers discipline our children, we don't stop loving them. On the contrary, we discipline *because* we love. Discipline out of anger or temper is unacceptable and borders on abuse.

93

Father God will often encourage us through discipline, because it's only the loved children of God who experience chastening: ' . . . the Lord disciplines those he loves, and he punishes everyone he accepts as a son.'[71]

Chastening is not getting even. As R. T. Kendall says, 'God got even at the cross.' Chastening comes rather to teach and direct us, and sometimes (when we're being stubborn) to shake us out of apathy and draw our hearts towards repentance. God has a number of methods available. Most often it will happen in private, just between God and us: as we open Scripture, the pure sword of the Spirit cuts through our arguments and hard-heartedness to the root of the issue. At other times, we experience a sense that God is drawing back from us: not to desert us, but rather to call us to go deeper and examine our hearts as we go.

Whatever method God chooses to use to chasten us, we should be assured of two things: we *shall* experience the chastening of the Lord at times, because we are loved of God. Secondly, whenever and however that happens, it's important to know that God is walking us through that solely and purely because we are so valuable to him. Obviously, God doesn't have off days like earthly fathers!

The Father who provides

Snapping his fingers and firing off an assortment of commands, the father swiftly makes sure that all the needs of the returned Prodigal are met. We'll look at these in detail later, but it's important to know here and now that while God is far more than an investment package, he is concerned and actively involved in providing the needs of life for his children.

'Can you afford this Mars bar, Dad?'

Most children have the ability to trust and receive from those they know. When I give Kelly, my daughter, a Mars bar, there is no sense of hesitation!

'Dad, are you sure you want me to have this? Perhaps I shouldn't take it. Have we paid the electricity bill?'

On the contrary, the chocolate disappears down her throat at the speed of light. Why? Because she lets me take care of all that complicated financial stuff. She finds it boring. She has never yet rushed in from school, planted a kiss on my cheek and cried, 'Well, Dad, let's talk mortgages, pensions and personal financial security, shall we?' (In fact both my children are so blissfully unaware of these things that they think their daddy is close to being a millionaire. Only time will relieve them of this most unfortunate illusion.)

While I find the 'God wants you to have a Rolls Royce' syndrome quite nauseating, I have found that God will provide gifts as well as needs. The gift itself is obviously very helpful, but there is an additional motive. With the gift comes encouragement, affirmation and a seal of approval. In that sense the gift becomes a token of the Father's love for us. Of course the gift always comes through human beings: God doesn't print banknotes!

When Kay and I planted a church in Peterborough, we had a vision, a strategy, and no money. I was in Bible college at the time, and so had to travel each weekend to take care of the new congregation. We needed a car. God spoke to our hearts very clearly, and assured us that we should not look for a car, for he had it all in hand. We waited.

It didn't take long for God to deliver. Two days later, an old friend whom I had not seen or spoken to for some years called us. He informed us that he had just had a new clutch and tyres fitted to his car. We weren't sure how to respond to this. Should we congratulate him concerning these mechanical developments in his life? In short, why on earth was he making a long-distance phone call to give us a health report on his vehicle?

He got to the point. 'The reason I'm telling you all this is because God spoke to me yesterday and told me that you need the car more than I do, and that I should give it to you. When will you be able to come and collect it?'

We were thrilled. Not only had God provided a car for us, but the way in which he did it warmed our hearts with a sense of security, confidence and confirmation. Just as a chocolate egg or a bunch of flowers every now and again encourages our children, so God loves to dispense liberal tokens of his deep affection for us.

'But I find it difficult to think of God as a Father'

If I had a pound for every time I have heard that complaint, I would be rather rich by now. Some of us have sadly endured being raised by domineering, uncaring, distant or abusive fathers. For those of us who have walked that pathway, even the word 'father' itself stabs and stings. We find it difficult to relax and feel at ease with the ultimate authority figure himself – God.

Others have been seriously damaged by religion. It

terrifies me to think that we get much of our understanding of what God is like from those who claim to
represent him – that is, speakers and preachers. If you
have 'sat under the ministry' ('cringed under the
bashing' is probably more accurate) of a Bible-punching
'screamer preacher' for any number of years, then you
will perhaps find it a struggle to relax in the presence of
God.

But it isn't only those with scars from upbringing or
religion who have problems with divine fatherhood. I
believe that most of us find it quite difficult really to
grasp the Father-heart of God. Perhaps you have
thought that you weren't quite normal because you've
found this difficult.

It's easy for us to carry the concept in our heads, but
the distance between the head and the heart can seem
like a billion miles. That's why the Holy Spirit has such a
major ministry in bringing assurance of God's fatherhood and family to us. 'The Spirit himself testifies with
our spirit that we are God's children.'[72] He himself is 'the
Spirit of sonship',[73] and the Bible says that it is 'by him
[the Holy Spirit] we cry "Abba, Father"'.

The theme is picked up again in Paul's letter to the
churches of Galatia: 'Because you are sons, God sent the
Spirit of his Son into our hearts, the Spirit who calls out
"Abba, Father."'[74]

As we allow the Holy Spirit to fill our lives we
discover a sense of confidence both in who God is –
Father – and in who we are – sons. (Sisters, don't send
me a parcel bomb. The term 'sons' in the Bible is a
neutral term, referring to male and female alike.)

Walk in the Spirit

In our daily life, as we walk in the Spirit[75] (walking relationally and with integrity with God), a growing sense of being parented develops. That's why I find speaking in tongues so helpful. Scripture shows us that when we speak in tongues, we edify ourselves.[76] As we speak, we gain boldness and confidence, because the Holy Spirit is, among other things, crying 'Abba', and the father-child relationship is enhanced. Like a child standing beside his seven-foot-tall daddy, we suddenly feel rather big when we know that God is more than at our side, he's within us by his Spirit.

Sometimes the Holy Spirit will lead us, whether we are conscious of it or not, to pray prayers that will specifically help that bonding process.

Share the incidental – like a green piano

I couldn't believe my ears. I had asked Louise, a member of our church in Peterborough, how I could pray for her. What did she need from the Lord? Her answer astonished me: 'I need a green piano.'

Louise and her husband Ian had recently moved into a house with a kitchen painted in a rather tasteful(!) green. Louise wanted a piano and she wanted to put it in the kitchen, so her preference was for a green piano.

Three weeks later, they were the owners of a green piano that had been given out of the blue – as it were. How many pianos of that particular colour are there in the world?

Louise had no theological theory as to why on earth God should be interested in the colour of a musical instrument. What she did have, and enjoys now, is a deep sense that God really is her Father. She often calls him 'Abba' in her prayers.

Ask God to take the garbage out

The Holy Spirit will also speak into our lives about the wounds and blockages that have accumulated through the years, blocking the Father's love.

Bitterness and a refusal to forgive will block out any sense of the love of God. It's so sad to see people who have been in church for years who are still nursing anger and resentment towards others.

'But I don't feel like forgiving,' we scream. Forgiveness is not a feeling – it's a choice. It is not an emotion, but an act of the will. However much we have been hurt or used, God still holds us accountable for our responses, because the ultimate victim of bitterness is always the one who is bitter.

This principle of accountability is graphically illustrated in the life of Michal, the wife of King David. Scripture describes a great day of celebration when the Ark of the Covenant was finally brought back to Jerusalem.[77] The city was filled with excitement. As the royal procession entered the city, the people blew trumpets and shouted at the top of their voices; sacrifices were offered every six steps along the way, and David was dancing with all his might! A colourful day, but Michal wasn't partying. The lady was watching the events from her window. She despised David, criticized his worship, and was effectively a big wet blanket on the whole day.

Now why did she act like that? Simple. She had been terribly hurt, particularly by men. When she met and fell in love with David, she told her father, King Saul. No congratulations came from Dad. On the contrary, he saw this relationship to be an ideal opportunity to trap David, and to use her as a snare to him.[78] Can you imagine the devastation of that?

So she married David, gained a husband, and felt used by her father.

After a while, Saul's campaign against David hotted up, David had to flee, and Michal was given in marriage to Paltiel.[79] Later, David returned home and wanted his wife back. She had to part from Paltiel and go home to David.[80] Her second husband followed her all the way, weeping and screaming.

Michal had been cruelly used by men almost all her life. No wonder she had become cynical and embittered. But God still held her accountable for her bitterness. As a result of her sarcastic attitude towards David and the Ark celebrations, she was struck barren, to the day of her death.[81]

Seems unfair? Not at all. God was demonstrating a vital principle: whatever the hurt of the past, we are still responsible to make sure that we respond with forgiveness. God loves us too much to let us get away with nursing emotional poison. The Holy Spirit will show us where there is a need for forgiveness so that the wound can be healed, and a fresh sense of life and 'sonship' will be ours.

Just in time

I saw this principle powerfully demonstrated a few years ago. I was preaching on forgiveness in a little church in Texas. In the congregation sat a man who was boiling with anger and bitterness. Many years earlier, he had been wrongly implicated in a Mafia-related crime.

He had served ten years, but though he was now free, he was still locked up in a cell of burning hatred towards the Mafia gunman who had given false evidence against him.

That night, he decided to end his years of anger. A choice was made to forgive. He wrote to the gunman, who was himself on death row for other crimes. He offered forgiveness, and shared the gospel with the man. I later discovered that, after ten long years, the letter arrived within two weeks of the gunman's scheduled execution.

Why drag around the excess baggage of hurts and anger from the past? God wants us to walk in freedom – and his fatherhood.

No slaves, only sons

The Prodigal had worked very hard on his 'make me a hired servant' speech, and began to deliver it just as he had planned. The father's response? He totally ignored it. No argument or debate, no room for negotiation, for the father could never envisage his child as a slave – only as a son.

Father ignored the speech, and immediately addressed the servants, 'Quick! Bring the best robe.' There's a wonderful impatience about it all – no time to be lost, for the son needs to be assured and affirmed. Every second that passes with the son feeling like a slave is a second too long.

God wants us to know his Fathercare . . . *now*. Ask him now to heal the hurts. Forgive those who've hurt you now. Share the little details of life today. Quick! There's a robe, a ring, a pair of shoes and a fattened calf waiting.

chapter five

The divine hug

He ran to his son, threw his arms around him and kissed him.

It wasn't so much his hair, matted with filth, or his shredded clothes that shocked; it was the hunted look in the boy's eyes that gripped the father's heart. He ran towards the boy as fast as his old legs would carry him, desperately trying to gulp air and call out his name all at the same time. Then he saw that look: pure fear. And even before they got close, the boy's voice rang out, something about 'not worthy', and 'hired servants'.

This was no time for words or long looks. There would be plenty of lingering conversation later. He threw himself at the boy, scooped him up in an embrace, and kissed his grubby cheeks. For a long time they stood there, wrapped up in each other, the boy's shoulders shaking as the tears flowed. At last, he took his son's hands in his own, stood back and looked into his eyes.

The hunted look was gone.

I'd like to get to know you well

Without question, Lloyd was one of the most unhappy-looking people I'd ever met. I was speaking at a youth weekend, and God seemed to be doing some good things, but Lloyd had the visage of a rather sick parrot throughout. I wondered what was wrong, so after the meeting was over, I decided to investigate.

'Excuse me . . . what's your problem?'

Lloyd began to tell me that his problem was with God. He was a Christian, but for some reason he got the jitters whenever the Holy Spirit began to move. The more God did, the more nervous he became.

We chatted, I prayed, and the next morning I looked across the meeting for Lloyd. There he was, looking more miserable than ever. So much for my counselling ministry.

Later in the meeting I asked folk to get into groups to pray. Lloyd joined a group, but shot me one of those 'I'd like to wallop you with a tactical nuclear warhead, brother' type looks that occasionally get sent in my direction during public meetings.

A few minutes passed with nothing but the murmur of prayer, and suddenly Lloyd broke out of his group and ran out of the room. 'That's it – too much pressure,' I thought, and made a mental note to follow up things after the meeting.

It was not to be the last we would see of Lloyd, however. Two minutes later he came back in, holding a fork. That's right, a fork! For a moment I thought he was mad with me, and that I was about to be the first martyr in the history of the church to be prodded to death, but now he was standing at the back of the hall, stabbing his left hand with the fork. I've seen some bizarre things happen in church meetings, but never had I seen anything like this.

At last, Lloyd came forward and asked if he could say a few words. He explained that he was a fireman, and that he had extensively damaged his left hand and wrist in an accident at work. The nerves in his wrist had been shattered, but the tendons worked. The result was that he had the full use of his hand, but no sensation. The doctors had told him that nothing could be done.

When he joined that group to pray, he made a sudden decision – he wanted to be able to let God come close, really close. In desperation, he had cried out to the Lord, and let all the barriers down. Suddenly, pain surged into his hand, as Jesus put all those shattered nerves back together. That's why he rushed out to get the fork, and was prodding his hand. He could scarcely believe the miracle that God had done.

Lloyd had said, 'God, come close.' God came close, and brought some healing with him.

More than anything else, God wants us to know his embrace. Relationship with him was the reason for the creation of humankind in the first place, and nothing is ever going to change that. That's why the picture of the Prodigal embraced by Dad is so important. It's much more than a pleasantly sentimental moment in the story.

I imagine that if Hollywood ever gave this parable a film treatment, this part of the story would make an ideal happy ending: the orchestra would be playing suitably tear-jerking music as son and Dad rush towards each other, in slow motion of course, like all the best toothpaste commercials. As they embrace in an even slower-motion hug, the camera zooms in on Dad's face, all relief and smiles. Then the screen goes misty at the edges as the camera picks up the Prodigal's tear-stained face. The orchestra goes insane and musicians apparently saw their violins in half as the frame is frozen, and the words 'The End' appear. Lights come up, and everyone dabs their eyes: 'Wasn't it lovely?'

But this is much more than a nice scene. As we consider the father hugging the breath out of his boy, the fact is that this is what God wants us to enjoy and prioritize – him. This embrace portrays the very heart of Christianity: the hug of God.

The boy needed other things. He needed new shoes. His stomach was empty. Cold and weary, he needed a good hot bath and some new clothes. But the father had another priority. Before he gave the boy anything, he gave him himself. All the other gifts followed quickly, but the first and most significant gift was the embrace.

Lest we become preoccupied with blessings rather than the Blesser himself, we'd do well to remember this simple principle: today and every day God's first word to us is, 'How about a hug, then?'

It's always been that way. Eden was paradise because God was there, strolling around in the cool of the day with Adam and Eve. Paradise wasn't made by a perfect climate or an absence of sickness or death. It was made by the fact that a full revelation and friendship with God were freely available. When the fall shattered that friendship, Eden became paradise lost.

Israel was significant during Old Testament times because God was among them; that's why the Tabernacle and the Ark of the Covenant were so important. The Ark was a specific reminder to the people that the living God had invested himself in them, not just blessing them or making them a people of destiny, but actually with them. In the case of the Ark, God was not in the box, but the box served as a constant reminder of the truth that God was in Israel. When Israel insisted that they needed a human king, because all the other nations had one, they effectively said, 'God isn't good enough.' They were the richest people in the world, but didn't know it. God had given them the greatest gift he has on offer: himself.

The same is true on the issue of our salvation, which was brought about by God once more giving himself. The shedding of animals' blood wasn't enough. When Jesus held out his hands and allowed nails to be hammered through them, God was saying, 'I give you myself. There isn't anything more precious, more valuable.'

A hug with God – that's what this Christianity is all about. As Jesus said before walking to the cross, 'This is eternal life: that they may know you, the only true God.'[82] And after the work was done, the veil in the temple was ripped from top to bottom by God; not from the bottom to the top by human beings. God was saying, 'Come close – not through your own efforts, but because I've ripped apart everything that would keep us distant. How about a hug?'

Less than the best

We often settle for less than that hug, less than God himself.

Church can become the focal point of our lives. I don't want to make too much of a distinction between God and God's church. The Lord doesn't deal with us as a group of scattered individuals; while he has a special relationship with each one of us, he relates to us as part of something bigger than we are. There is no room for the 'me and my personal Jesus' syndrome that has particularly pervaded the American culture. Having made that point, it is none the less possible to become, as Tozer put it, 'preoccupied with Christianity rather than Christ'. Perversely, this is particularly true if you are part of an excellent church.

The programme is varied, the preaching interesting and relevant, relationships strong and time-consuming. Wonderful, that's how church is meant to be. Boring, building-centred Christianity is a scandal.

The down side is that we can lean so hard upon church that we neglect our own personal walk with God. Cancel a few preaching and teaching meetings in some churches and you'll see what I mean. 'You can't do that. The word must be preached, the people must be fed.' The implication is that the teaching programme of the local church is to be the primary source of our spiritual nourishment. Not so! The only people who legitimately 'need to be fed' are in prams! We're to be responsible for our own spiritual nourishment. Church alone is insufficient. Hear Tozer:

but what about "feed my sheep?"

> Right now we are in an age of religious complexity. The simplicity which is in Christ is rarely found among us. In its stead are programmes, methods, organisations and a world of nervous activities which occupy time and attention but can never satisfy the longing of the heart.[83]

Church can become a substitute for God, and (fasten you seat-belts) so can the truth, but the truth of Scripture is to lead us to the God who lives. The Bible is God's word to us, but we worship the Giver, not the gift. Correct information and truth become our priority, so we stick the pulpit right in the middle of the church building, because in our fellowship 'the word is central'. (Actually, what is meant is that the *preaching* is central.) Sounds very pious, but I thought that Jesus himself was supposed to be at the centre of everything? The Bible is the only infallible source of information *about* God since he inspired it, but God is not the Bible.

Our addiction to information is evidenced by the fact that we pack potential leaders off to Bible colleges so that they can gather even more information in order to prepare themselves for Christian ministry. Heads full of theory, but with no functional experience or opportunity to learn 'on the job', the graduates rush out of the academic cloisters, now allegedly equipped for leadership. Instead of allowing leadership to emerge in local churches, and shaping, training, and giving local opportunity as well as information, we make the ability to accumulate data the criterion for leadership.

Of course we need Scripture: the Bible is the only infallible source of truth about God. Without it we'll get stuck on subjective quicksand. But God is more than a concept, a doctrine or a theory. Christianity is more than a package of precepts. God is a Person, not a principle. He lives, speaks, is active, loves, laughs and he *is*!

We have to allow this living God to get a hold of us (and of course often that will be as we read Scripture, though not exclusively), otherwise our Christianity will degenerate into a slavish adherence to a beautifully true ideology.

The kingdom rather than the King

For those who are really keen to do something for God, another subtle temptation awaits. It's possible to become so preoccupied with ministry and service that you lose sight of God in it all – the kingdom becomes larger than the King. We work *for* God rather than *with* God. There's a massive difference.

Frantically rushing from evangelistic pillar to pastoral post, we breathe a quick 'Bless what I'm about to do, Lord. I hope you're in it somewhere' prayer, and then wonder why we feel disillusioned, burnt out and cynical.

A vivid illustration of this is found in Peter's life. He was asleep in Gethsemane when the gang turned up to arrest Jesus, Judas as their leader. Peter had been told to pray, but he fell asleep; he was unprepared for the stressful event that took place. He woke up, pulled out his sword, rushed across the garden, and cut off the High Priest's servant's ear.

Can you see that in your imagination? Peter stood there, sleep still in his eyes, sword in one hand, bloody ear in the other, and of course Jesus didn't say anything; but perhaps his eyes said: 'Well, Peter, that was a very helpful thing to do. Thank you very much for your input.' Peter was doing his own thing for God, and ears were amputated as a result.

Those of us who are busily involved in serving God need to remember that we're sons and daughters before we're servants. God isn't overly impressed with the size and influence of our ministry. Rather, it's our relationship and friendship with him that he values most. That's where our security and motivation have to come from.

I was holding meetings in a church on the border between America and Mexico, and was spending the afternoon in prayer and preparation for the evening meeting. My requests were fairly predictable. I asked God to bless the people, save the unsaved, encourage the weary . . .

Suddenly, I sensed God saying, 'Why do you want me to do all that?'

Not an amazingly intelligent question, I thought.

'It's obvious. I want to see your glory, see people helped, blah blah . . .'

God simply said, 'Don't you ever try to find your security from your ministry.'

I realized that my sense of well-being so often hinged on how well I spoke, and whether or not people responded. When I ministered, the biggest thing at stake was my ego.

God was showing me that security must come from my friendship with him alone. In the space of about fifteen seconds, two biblical incidents flashed into my mind that graphically illustrated the point; both incidents in the life of Jesus.

The first was his baptism, when the Father shouted from heaven. This was the beginning of the Messiah's public ministry – an ideal opportunity for the voice to say, 'Listen, chaps, this is the Redeemer of planet Earth. He can heal the sick and raise the dead, so open up your little ears. This is the greatest ministry that the world has ever seen.'

A heavenly endorsement of Jesus' ministry would have been helpful, but the voice didn't mention ministry at all. Rather, Father hollered from heaven his excitement about his relationship with Christ: 'You are my Son, whom I love; with you I am well pleased.'[84]

The second moment was the transfiguration – the other time that the voice rang out. Now it's near to crucifixion day. A few sentences of approval and explanation about the Saviour's ministry would not have gone amiss, and perhaps might have helped the trembling disciples. So what does Father say? 'This is my Son; hear him!' Father gets so excited that he tears the heavens open and speaks into our world, and it's *relationship* that stirs his heart – not ministry.

Paul knew something about that priority. Writing to his friends at Philippi he states his great ambition: 'I want to know Christ.'[85] The hug was the most important issue in Paul's life – not service. That's why God could trust Paul with such a major, massively significant ministry: intimacy with Christ had priority over service. Like David, he was a man after God's heart, because he was always running after the heart of God. 'My soul thirsts for you, my body longs for you, in a dry and weary land where there is no water.'[86]

Time to put on the tin helmet and run for cover

Are you getting nervous? Perhaps you're waiting for me to mention that dreaded subject guaranteed to make even the strongest heart tremble: *the quiet time.*

Most evangelicals believe in the quiet-time concept. From some, however, one definitely gets the impression that there is a scale of spirituality that centres around this supposed daily phenomenon.

Class A spirituality is reserved for Mother Teresa, Billy Graham and those who have an hour of prayer each morning *before* 6am. Extra points can be earned for a further half-hour spent reading the Bible in (a) the original languages or (b) the King James Version, which, for some of us, is just as hard to understand as (a).

Class B are the folk who spend half an hour in prayer and Bible study at any time during the day. Points should be deducted for praying while riding your bike, having a bath or during anything else that's enjoyable. Your score will also be reduced if you read from the Living Bible or any version with pictures or cartoons in it.

Class C is reserved for those who pray only when they feel like it, which frequently means when they are (a) broke, (b) thinking about changing job, (c) bored with what's on the TV. These folk are ploughing through either *Every Other Day with Jesus* (the companion volume to the great classic *Once in a While with God*) or their *Once Through the Bible in 500 Years* course.

There are other people, of course, who passionately believe in the quiet-time idea . . . but don't ever have one. Mind you, they get very upset if anyone suggests that God still likes us even on the days when we miss the QT.

'You ought to be ashamed of yourself'

A well-known preacher was waxing eloquent on the issue of religiosity in general and quiet times in particular. Not a few evangelical sacred cows were being ushered to the slaughterhouse that night. Suddenly, right in the middle of the sermon, a man in the congregation stood to his feet.

113

'You ought to be ashamed of yourself, young man! You should be telling these people to get up every morning at 6am for prayer and Bible study. This is *disgusting*!'

Understandably, the place went rather quiet . . . until the heckler's wife piped up: 'Why do you say that? *You* never do it.'

It's no good passionately believing in an idea but never living by it. That which we *really* believe, we live by. All the rest is religious froth.

So what about prayer? Without a doubt, prayer will be the place where we really feel God's hug. Let's face a few facts about prayer.

'God, save that duck!': yes, prayer is difficult

There's an old hymn that talks about the 'sweet hour of prayer'. While it's true that prayer can be one of the great adventures of life, prayer is often quite difficult. The hour (or seven minutes) is not so sweet when you feel as though you're smacking your head against a brick wall.

It's difficult to hold a conversation with someone we can't physically see, hear or touch. All kinds of very visible, touchable demands scream for our attention. When we do get to be still for a while, our minds have a tendency to wander. (Right in the middle of our heartfelt intercession for Malaysia, we wonder what's for tea.)

Or we fall asleep. This frequently happens to me when I try to pray in bed, which is often. It's early in the morning. The previous night, having read a dynamic work on intercession, Smith Wigglesworth, or revival, feeling very spiritual and slightly unearthly, I set my alarm clock for some unearthly hour. The best intentions were in my heart when I set that clock: I would arise, stir my heart, exercise, make a cup of tea for my wife, and . . . pray!

About six hours later, the alarm clock has what appears to be a violent fit. Staggered at the amount of hatred that a rational human being can have towards an inanimate object like a clock, I slap it into silence. Then I remember, it's time to pray.

But . . . it's cold out there in the bleakness of my bedroom. I know, I'll stay in bed, cocooned in the warm blankets, and pray. After all, doesn't the Bible say something about meditating on the Lord *on your bed*? (It's amazing how many times I've recalled that scripture early in the morning when I don't want to get up. It's a handy little quote.)

I start to pray, and for a while things go well. But my mind, barely awake and lulled again by the cosy bed, begins to drift. I'm still praying, but I'm half asleep.

When you're almost asleep, your power of logic is weak. You think strange things. If you're trying to pray in this state, you will pray strange things too. One morning, I was in this coma/prayer state, and Disneyland came into my mind. I started to pray for Disneyland, home of Donald Duck, Mickey Mouse and others . . . and then it happened. I sat bolt upright in bed, and yelled out passionately: 'Oh God, save that duck!'

Yes, prayer is difficult, and God knows that. That's why the Holy Spirit inspired Paul to write to the church at Rome, 'We do not know what we ought to pray.'[87] It's good to know that, otherwise we shall not only struggle with prayer at times, but we'll feel abnormal and condemned, as if we're the only ones who find it difficult. Then we go round in circles on the issue.

Great commitments to prayer are made after reading an inspiring book on the subject, or hearing a great sermon. We determine to pray more, find it tough, get discouraged, and so don't pray, until the next sermon or book, when we get inspired again . . .

Prayer: down with legalism, long live discipline!

Some have reacted against the quiet-time idea, dismissing the habit of daily prayer as being legalistic. In many ways, they're right. There are many of us who don't feel worthy unless we've put some time in for God, which is legalistic. God loves us because we're his children, not because we spend a certain amount of time earning his love.

The reaction against legalism, however, can be equally unhelpful. I heard one leader say recently, 'Don't pray because you have to . . . pray when you want to.' It sounds like a nice idea, but it is actually very unhelpful. We don't apply that kind of advice to any other necessity of life. Some things should be done because they are important, however we may feel about them. You might not feel like taking a shower or cleaning your teeth for a week, but necessity (and the maintenance of friendships) demands that you do it anyway, regardless of your feelings.

All relationships, including our friendship with God, are nurtured by choices, not feelings. That's why the Bible commands us to love our wives, husbands and neighbours. Feelings aren't the final authority – what is right is. In Hollywood, people fall in love. In the Bible, people walk in love. There's a world of difference.

Prayer is vital. As M. C. Hammer says, 'We've got to pray – just to make it today.' I need the Father's help to

116

preach and minister, and to respond correctly to my children, help with the washing-up and a host of other ordinary things that are part of everyday life. Choices have to be made.

We don't need legalism, but we *do* need discipline. There's a big difference. Legalism is about motives ('I pray because I want God to love me'); discipline is about making what is right happen. ('I know God loves me, I want to get to know him more, therefore I will pray.')

Paul hated legalism. Coming from the pharisaic background that he did, he loathed the idea of 'buying God'. Read the letter to the church at Galatia if you're not convinced. At one point he declared that he would like the religious legalists in Galatia to castrate themselves![88] You couldn't get a clearer denunciation of legalism than that.

But while he utterly rejected legalism, he was committed to discipline in his daily life. He knew that he had within him the tendency to love what was wrong and shy away from what was right: 'What I want to do I do not, but what I hate I do.'[89] So this anti-legalistic campaigner engaged in discipline in his own personal life. He determined that he was going to control his body, rather than allow himself to be controlled: 'I beat my body and make it my slave.'[90]

Writing to Timothy, he reminded the young man that 'God did not give us a spirit of timidity, but of . . . self-discipline'.[91]

The late David Watson was committed to this pathway of non-legalistic discipline. He wrote:

I have never found it easy getting up in the morning to pray! Virtually every day is a real battle; but because I believe it to

117

be a battle worth winning, I have taken active and practical steps to 'pommel my body and subdue it!' For many years I have used two alarms to wake me up, since I sometimes find that one on its own will fail to wake me. In the early days . . . I used to have one alarm clock by my bed, then another cheap but very noisy alarm outside my door set to go off ten minutes after the first. Because the second alarm would wake the whole household (and make me thoroughly unpopular), I had some motivation to get out of bed as soon as the first alarm had sounded. This scheme never failed! In many ways, I am ashamed to have to resort to such methods when rising to pray means rising to enjoy the Great Lover; nevertheless I am grateful to those who helped me to see that this is an important daily battle to take seriously and win![92]

Be practical about your praying. I have a simple cure for my sleeping/prayer problem: I walk and pray. (It's quite difficult to fall asleep while you're walking along the street.)

Whatever time you choose to pray, and whatever posture you choose, you will have to make a decision about it daily. Yesterday's discipline and commitment aren't enough.

You will need discipline in programming prayer (actually finding some time to pray), and you will need to be disciplined as you pray. In a society where everything is instantly available (fast food, instant coffee, remote-control TVs and the rest) prayer stands as a challenge to our hunger for everything *now*!

Just as an aeroplane has the capacity to go through the sound barrier, so I have discovered that in prayer I have to break through the 'flesh barrier'. Don't read too much into my words. I'm not suggesting that at some point I break 'into the Spirit' and pop off through the ozone layer to another plane of spiritual awareness. Rather, it often takes me about twenty minutes (often just spent worshipping, particularly speaking in tongues) for me to concentrate my thinking and begin to move in to a greater depth of prayer.

A word about the Word

Most Christians believe that the normal Christian life will involve daily Bible reading. It *is* good to allow pure truth to fill your mind, but that won't be accomplished by merely reading (or, as often happens, running your tired eyes over black print at the end of another exhausting day). Bible reading can become like the rosary. We discover that our reading for the day is four chapters of Leviticus. It doesn't look that inspiring – blood and kidneys appear to be sailing all over the place, and due to the fact that your ox hasn't gored your neighbour's ox lately, it doesn't appear to be that relevant. But, we tell ourselves, we must do the Bible reading. So we hurriedly allow our eyes to run through the four chapters in about three minutes, then lay the Bible aside, satisfied that we've read the Word for the day.

Actually, we've achieved nothing. We are commanded to *feed* on the Word, not read it. That means we think about it (meditate), commit ourselves to it (swallow) and memorize it (digestion).

Be careful about throwing open the Bible in order 'to get something from God'. God is gracious, so in the early stages of our Christian lives many of us have done the Bible lucky dip, and God has spoken. That shouldn't set a pattern for the future, however. You can get yourself into serious confusion by using Scripture in this way.

A man once picked up his King James Bible, desperate to hear from God. He closed his eyes, opened the Bible, plonked his finger down on it, and found an inspiring verse, which said, 'And Judas went and hanged himself.' With a nervous laugh, he decided to try again. That couldn't be a word from God to him, could it? The next attempt set his heart racing. His finger landed on, 'Go and do thou likewise.' The third attempt did little to calm his fears: 'What thou doest, do quickly.'

Towards tomorrow

Lay aside your list of needs for a moment. Put aside your guilty feelings about not being able to pray as you'd like to. If you're only praying for a couple of minutes a day, don't tell yourself that as from tomorrow, you're going to wake at 3am and spend five hours in prayer and study before going to work. You'll miss the target, become discouraged, and be back where you started. It's better to decide to take five or ten minutes a day specifically to pray, and hit the target. Learning to pray is like learning to ride a bike – the more you do it, the easier it becomes.

I've tried to be very honest. Prayer, and feeding on Scripture, can be the most exhilarating thrill; it can also be incredibly hard work. But when we commit ourselves to the hug of God, suddenly this Christianity begins to make sense. Without it, we become exhausted followers of a moral code, religious people rather than people of relationship. The hug is the source of everything.

Noel Richards puts it like this:

I know how much it hurts him, every time we run
away,
Ignoring His existence, cos it's easier that way.
Though we try to live without Him, from this fact
we cannot hide,
God is a loving Father, whose love for us won't die,
And we need him in our lives.

He will not reject you, when you tell him what
you've done.
He knows the truth about us, and what we have
become.
He welcomes us with open arms, although we
cause Him pain,
Forgiving our unfaithfulness, he takes away our
shame.
He's so glad we're home again . . .

God could find no other way of making you His
child;
His only Son was punished, for the wrong you've
done He died.
So do not turn your back on Him, but look into the
face
Of one who cares so much for you and wants to
keep you safe.
No, do not turn your back on him, but look into the
face
Of one who cares so much for you and wants to
keep you safe,
In the strength of his embrace.

Father's love, Father's love,

No-one loves us like the Father does.
Father's love, Father's love,
We all need the Father's love.

chapter six

Fully forgiven

But the father said to his servants, 'Quick! Bring the best robe and put it on him. Put a ring on his finger and sandals on his feet. Bring the fatted calf and kill it. Let's have a feast.'

The boy looked into his eyes and spoke. 'Father, I'm not worthy . . . make me one of your hired servants.' There was a long silence, as Father considered what best to say. How could he convince his son that everything really was all right? What words would bring the assurance that was so needed?

Then he saw it: he would say nothing, for no words could ever fully communicate what was in his heart. He would *show* his son his response. Actions could speak what words could never say.

The servants were sweating by now. They knew that the master was impatient. One rushed forward, his arms laden down with beautiful clothes. Another came with shoes. Still another, bearing a glittering ring on a cushion.

He watched his son's eyes widen with amazement. How much he wanted the boy to understand that he was forgiven. Would he get the message?

Rich man, poor man . . . lotteries are big business in America. If you happen to be the fortunate one in twenty million, you may well walk off with a fortune. The prizes are massive.

Several years ago, a man won the lottery, but he didn't know it. Some $18 million were waiting to be claimed, but the man with the winning ticket had gone off into the wilderness to hunt for a couple of weeks. Sitting in his pocket was a piece of paper potentially worth a fortune, but there was a time limit set for the claim, so people were out hunting for the hunter, frantically trying to find him so that he wouldn't lose the cash. The hope was that someone would discover him in the woods, grab hold of his shoulders and say, 'Don't you know – *you're rich*!' I don't know if they found him in time.

If you're a Christian, I want you to know that God has bestowed upon you the gift of forgiveness, and he wants you to walk in the good of that right now. In that sense, you're rich! Tragically, I have discovered that there are thousands of Christians who walk around under clouds of condemnation and false guilt. Like the man in the woods, they have everything, but nothing.

The video syndrome

I'm not talking about those who are experiencing the gentle conviction of the Holy Spirit for present sin. As we've already seen, repentance is the only solution for that kind of guilt. I'm addressing the people who have made a mistake, perhaps a serious one, in the past, and they have truly repented. In fact, they've repented more times than they can remember. Everything is fine for a while; they know that they've been forgiven . . . until a preacher mentions that specific sin in a sermon. Alarm bells start to go off, and waves of condemnation flood into the mind. They repent again and everything is fine . . . until a few days later, perhaps during a time of prayer or while reading Scripture, the condemnation comes again.

It's like a video replay of your sin going on in your mind, over and over again, and there's something incredibly ironic about the 'video syndrome'. Very often it's the Christians who really are keen to live all out for God who suffer from this the most. They want to be totally committed to Christ, so they're the ideal victims for this kind of mental torture.

Confusion begins to fill their hearts. Is this God speaking to me? (This is compounded by the fact that the 'video replays' often take place during church meetings, particularly during a 'hot' sermon.) Discouragement follows. Why live for God today when they are struggling with excess baggage from the past? Who wants to worship God with enthusiasm when they feel like a piece of trash?

The replays work with special devastation when some form of sexual sin has been committed. Somehow it seems harder to accept forgiveness when something lurid and furtive has taken place that makes you blush when you remember it.

Whatever the sin, the replays can blind you for years. I know what I'm talking about. Just after I became a Christian, I committed a particular sin. I watched video replays of that sin in my mind for about seven years. I apologized to God, perhaps a thousand times. I would cry during church meetings, but still no relief came. Why wouldn't God forgive me?

Then one day I learned that God *had* forgiven me, the very moment I had repented. There was someone running a video player in my mind, but it wasn't God. The finger on the remote-control button belonged to the devil.

Let me spell it out to you: if you have genuinely repented from that episode in your past, but still suffer from the agony of condemnation, then hear this, and hear it well. God is not convicting you. Satan is condemning you.

The Bible describes Satan as the 'accuser of our brothers'[93] as well as the author of temptation.[94] He comes with a twofold attack. *Temptation* is designed to encourage sin in the present. *Condemnation* is useful to him because it brings us into false guilt because of sins of the past. Both weapons are devastating. To feel guilty about today, or to have your face rubbed in yesterday's failures, the result is the same: dejection.

In one sense, it's nothing personal. Satan hates Jesus and all that he stands for. The cross was the place where our forgiveness was legally purchased, and Satan's rights over us were legally smashed. The work of the cross stands complete, for ever. There is nothing that the Enemy can do to reverse or undo what Jesus did there. It is complete, finished!

But while the Enemy cannot touch what Jesus did, he can affect our experience and enjoyment of what Jesus accomplished.

God says, 'You're forgiven.'

Satan says, 'Oh yes? Do you *feel* forgiven?'

In many ways, the Enemy has an easy time. The fact is that most of us human beings struggle with free gifts – we always want to pay our way. Try giving someone a present or special gift when it *isn't* their birthday or Christmas. Lots of people squirm: 'Oh, you shouldn't have. Let me pay you. I feel awful.'

We want to pay. That's why people will happily light candles, do penance, and, in some religions, walk on hot coals or put spears through their noses in order to gain forgiveness.

God says, 'I want to forgive you', and we, in a twisted form of pride, say, 'No, let me pay you.' It goes without saying that the Enemy doesn't really have to work overtime to have us self-sufficient humans wallowing in a pool of condemnation.

Perhaps what I've described has been happening to you. You're not alone. As I have spoken on this subject in various parts of the world, I've seen literally tens of thousands of Christians respond because of the 'video syndrome'.

God has gone to an incredible amount of effort to enable us to experience the quiet peace that comes when we know we really are forgiven. So what is the way forward, out of this mental journey that we have made perhaps hundreds of times?

We need to understand the nature and scope of God's amazing forgiveness. It's the truth that sets us free.

The Father initiates forgiveness

'Quick!' he barks, and sends the servants scurrying. There is a sense of loving impatience here; not a second should be lost. Enough time has been wasted; now it's time for the Prodigal to become a son again in the fullest sense of the word.

We must understand that God's forgiveness is

initiated by him, it's his idea! He has made all the necessary arrangements, sending Jesus to a cross to pay for our sins legally. That's why Scripture declares, 'If we confess our sins, he [God] is faithful [that means he *always* forgives] and just [that means it's *legally correct* for him to pardon us] and will forgive us our sins.'[95]

The price was paid, as one singer puts it, 'paid on the nail'. Forgiveness is not God winking at our sin, carelessly saying, 'Oh all right, I'll let you get away with it this time.' The bill has been settled, at Father's command. Right now God is eager for us to walk in the truth of that. I have seen God go to some quite extraordinary measures to get his children to understand that.

A very specific word of knowledge

I was taking part in a large meeting with about 800 young people, and a friend, Gary Mitchell, came to the platform and shared that God had given him some specific information about someone in the crowd (a word of knowledge). Apparently there was a young woman there who had aborted her baby some years earlier, but was now experiencing the 'video syndrome'. God had told Gary the day, month and year that the baby was aborted, because he wanted the girl to be set free from her guilt and condemnation.

What an amazing God! At the end of the meeting, the young lady came forward for prayer, somewhat bewildered, but amazed by the love of God. Like the Prodigal, she had heard Father say: 'Quick!'

The price has been paid for us to be forgiven, and on that basis God declares us clean. Who are we to argue?

We react like Peter did when God showed him a vision of all kinds of animals that any Jew would have called unclean.[96] But God was doing a new thing, and told Peter, 'Do not call anything impure that God has made clean.'[97]

I want to put it forcefully: God says you're clean. How dare you say otherwise!

An offence to our pride

The Father brought out a robe and had it put on his son's shoulders. The Greek word used here means 'a stately robe', a long garment reaching to the feet, or with a train behind. It was this kind of garment that the scribes used to wear to make themselves conspicuous![98] That's why some translators say that the servants brought out the *best* robe.

Imagine how the scribes who were standing in the crowd reacted when Jesus had the father draping the stole on his son's shoulders! They wore their robes in order to make a religious fashion statement about their personal piety. The scribes's robe represented earned righteousness. And here is a returned pigpen hand being given a robe just like theirs! What an outrage – he didn't deserve such an honour!

Exactly. The Prodigal deserved punishment, rebuke and, at best, a bed in the servants' quarters. But he got the best robe.

Forgiveness is based on the grace (unmerited favour) of God. Grace strikes a death blow to human pride, because there's absolutely nothing we can do to earn it. To most of us that comes as a tremendous relief, but there is still something in us that says, 'No, I want to pay!' That's why the cross is an offence to the human mind.[99] The word 'offence' is *skandalon*, which means literally 'scandal'.

God says, 'I forgive you.' Human pride says 'Scandalous!'

God says, 'There's nothing you can do. It's all done.' Human pride says, 'Scandalous!'

No wonder this grace is called 'amazing'!

Forgiveness: dry the tears

Having brought out the best robe, the servants rush to bring shoes to the son, and they are told, 'Put . . . sandals on his feet.' The boy stood there helpless, the servants fumbled with the thongs of the sandal, and a powerful statement was being made.

The Prodigal was home, and at that moment he had no use for shoes or sandals. Shoes were always removed when entering either houses or sacred buildings, because they had been in contact with 'common ground'. So why did Dad break out the sandals?

These shoes weren't made for walking – they were to teach the boy that his time of mourning and sadness was over for good. In Bible days it was common practice to remove the shoes as a sign of repentance for sin. 'Take off your sandals,' God said to Moses, 'for the place where you are standing is holy ground.'[100] Joshua was given the same instruction by the angel of the Lord.[101]

When the father handed out new sandals, he was saying, 'Wipe your tears away, son. Stop weeping about the past. Your dignity is restored.'

So shoes were given, and they were placed on his feet by servants. The father was honouring the boy. It was common in Bible days to honour someone with the words, 'I'm not worthy to untie his sandals.' John the Baptist spoke those very words about Jesus.[102] As the servants set about their humble work, the son was realizing that he could never be a mere servant in his father's eyes. Only sons could receive treatment like this.

Perhaps you've been filled with remorse about your past; God wants you to have shoes of dignity and honour on your feet again. To those of us with downcast eyes, he comes as our 'Glorious One, who lifts up my head'.[103]

Forgiveness: authority restored

It was like Christmas. The best robe, a new pair of sandals, and then a ring was placed upon his finger. The ring was a symbol of authority, and meant that the boy was now able to give orders in his father's name. In Old Testament times people often had a seal built into a ring that could be used to authenticate documents: thus Pharaoh honoured Joseph as prime minister of Egypt when he took off his signet ring and placed it on Joseph's finger.[104] Joseph now had authority in the name of Pharaoh. The evil Haman was given the full authority of King Xerxes when the king 'took his signet ring from his finger and gave it to Haman'.[105]

The forgiveness of God restores us to a place of full authority in the name of Jesus. We carry his authority, not our own. 'In the name of Jesus' is more than an orthodox formula to conclude a prayer; it is the fruit of God's pardon upon our lives. Confident in the forgiveness of God, we can take authority in a number of areas.

Under our feet

We now have authority over the accuser, the devil. We don't have to put up with the insidious whispers and hints that he brings. We can take authority over Satan in a way that even the angels themselves have never enjoyed. Even the angel Michael couldn't himself rebuke Satan;[106] rather, he had to say, 'The Lord rebuke you.'

Why? Because Michael was an angel of lesser rank than Satan, who had held an incredibly high authority before his plummet from heaven.

But we as the people of God have been given a ring of authority by Jesus, and so *we* resist the devil, and he flees from *us*.[107] Notice, he runs, not from Jesus, but from us. We must never forget that our authority is only in and through the work of Jesus, and our power comes from the Holy Spirit in us ('The one who is in you is greater than the one who is in the world').[108] Notwithstanding that, we have a ring on our finger to overcome the one who brings false guilt!

Now how do we take authority? Scripture helps us here. When the Enemy whispers accusation, we can overcome him by using two weapons. The book of Revelation reveals that we are overcomers through 'the blood of the Lamb and the word of our testimony'.

The first overcoming weapon, then, is 'the blood of the Lamb'.[109] What does that mean? Often you will hear people using the formula, 'We cover [the person, situation, whatever] with the blood of the Lamb.' Frankly, I'm not sure that this is a helpful way to pray. The idea is being picked up from the Exodus account where blood was placed on the door posts and the lintels of houses. God said, 'When I see the blood, I will pass over you.'[110] But the blood of Christ has been shed, once and for all, and now it is that blood that 'purifies us from every sin'.[111]

The word 'purifies' is in the present continuous tense, so we can say, 'The blood keeps on continually purifying us.' When Satan accuses, we overcome as we state that the price has already been paid by the shed blood. Don't argue that *you* are righteous; state that *he* is righteous, and you're in him! Like a child who is totally unafraid of a school bully, because his big brother is around, so realize that you can boast about the work of your big brother, Jesus.

The second weapon is 'the word of our testimony'. Scripture also declares that we overcome 'by the word of [our] testimony'.[112] Forgiveness enables us to know who we are in God – that's why the New Testament is so full of powerful statements about our position in Christ: 'We are children of God';[113] 'We are more than conquerors.'[114]

These truths are not written to make us feel nice: gushing words from a sentimental God. Rather, they are to equip us with an understanding that the authority of God has been invested in us, and we stand in him.

Jesus overcame Satan by declaring Scripture; the Word of God is the sword of the Spirit. As Christ said, 'It is written!' three times in the wilderness, the devil was cut to the quick.

Declare Scripture when you feel accused. The price has been paid, and Scripture is the receipt – so show the man the receipt!

As Jack Hayford says, 'The devil is a liar, and one day he will go to the lake of fire. So next time the devil tries to remind you about your past, go ahead and remind him about his future!'

Arrest that thought!

There's one further area where we need to exercise

authority, and that's over ourselves – and particularly over our minds.

The Bible clearly teaches us that we can control our thinking. Paul encourages the Philippians to think on that which is true, right, noble, pure and admirable.[115] God doesn't command us to do what is beyond our reach. With the help of the Holy Spirit we can control our thinking. 'We take captive every thought to make it obedient to Christ,' says Paul.[116] The word 'captive' in that verse means 'to bring under control'. We're not called to be at the mercy of any stray thought that might happen to pop into our heads. The 'video syndrome' is a mental journey, a battle fought, won or lost in our minds. We can refuse to go on that journey.

Be bold about it. You don't have to go around in mental circles, rehearsing yesteryear's sins. Take authority over the Enemy – and yourself.

No wonder we worship

The Pharisees and teachers of the law murmured among themselves. This was dangerous teaching! They were the ones who would drag a woman caught in adultery into a public setting and use her as an item for debate: no regard for human dignity, no compassion or forgiveness. Principle blazed in their hearts, but, tragically, love was cremated in the process.

For the sinners, however, there was hope, encouragement, mercy. God seemed to be opening his arms to them as Jesus spoke.

Whatever your history, the arms are open for you. The father worked overtime to help the Prodigal understand his forgiveness. Do you get it?

chapter seven

The father who celebrates

'Bring the fattened calf and kill it. Let's have a feast and celebrate. For this son of mine was dead and is alive again; he was lost and is found.' So they began to celebrate.

The warm candlelight gave an almost magical glow to the whole event. What a night! Laughter blended into the blur of many conversations as dinner was served. The beef didn't disappoint: it was exquisite.

As the wine flowed, the musicians began their work, and soon the old house was alive with dancing. Now, as he stood outside in the moonlight, a brief rest for him as the celebrations continued, the father marvelled. His son was home. Alive, and well.

How many times had he tossed and turned through the night, fearful that his boy might have been injured, or killed? But that was yesterday. Now he had come home. The household was complete again.

Wiping away a stray tear, he went back inside.

God enjoys a good party. Notice I use the term 'good'. Obviously, I'm not talking about the sort of affair where moral judgment deteriorates as alcohol intake escalates. Those aren't good, or, for that matter, much fun.

But the God of the Bible is clearly someone who knows what it is to laugh, celebrate, dance for joy and generally have a good time. Like the father in this parable, he gets excited about his children rather easily. Zephaniah has been described as 'the prophet obsessed with doom', but even he talks about the God who will 'take great delight' in his people and who will 'rejoice over [them] with singing'.[117] The word 'rejoice' there literally means 'to leap'.

Whenever someone becomes a Christian, it's party time in heaven. Two minutes before telling the parable of the Prodigal, Jesus told the crowd that there is 'rejoicing in the presence of the angels of God over one sinner who repents'.[118] I used to think that meant the *angels* did the rejoicing, but that's not what it says. The rejoicing happens *in their presence*. Perhaps that means God himself is the One who is doing most of the celebrating!

And in this parable, as Jesus paints a portrait of Father God, it's Dad himself who says, 'Let's party!' He's been waiting for an excuse – the fattened calf is standing by.

Folk in Old Testament times had some unbelievable parties too. Once a year, they had an incredible blow-out in Jerusalem. The people took 10% of their earnings to the temple, and spent the lot on the celebration! Listen to these words from Deuteronomy: 'Use the silver to buy whatever you like: cattle, sheep, wine or other fermented drink, or anything else you wish.'[119]

That can't be in the Bible! Believe me, it is! The idea was to bring everybody together, whatever their background or status, for a gigantic carnival event. Tons of food, lakes of wine, lots of dancing and laughter – and all in the name of God.

Then Jesus came, declaring that those who saw him saw the Father. And he lived a life that made the boring brigade mad. Yes, he was the 'man of sorrows', but he also knew how to tell a funny story. (The idea of a camel passing through the eye of a needle doesn't strike me as incredibly funny, but I'm told that the average 2,000-year-old Hebrew would think it hysterical.)

He was a popular party guest, and not just because he could make excellent wine out of water in a second. (The equivalent of 914 70cl bottles at Cana!) Everyone was jealous when Zacchaeus hosted him for lunch; and little children, who would instinctively run a mile from a grey, wild-eyed ascetic, just flocked to him. He lived the abundant life that he proclaimed.

He didn't enjoy miseries who acted like wet blankets at parties. At a dinner given in his honour, Jesus had perfume poured over his feet by Mary, who then wiped his feet with her hair. Judas, the omnipresent killjoy, protested very loudly. Accusations of extravagance were thrown around; the perfume was worth a year's wages. But Jesus sided with Mary, and announced that she would be for ever remembered because of what she did.

Jesus enjoyed celebrations so much that the Pharisees called him a 'glutton and a drunkard, a friend of tax collectors and "sinners"'.[120] Unlike those who never have any legitimate fun for fear that they might offend, Jesus enjoyed life and laughter even though the religious people screamed their criticisms.

When asked what the kingdom of God was like, Jesus used, among other illustrations, the picture of a wedding party.[121]

And the future? It's like yet another wedding party – the marriage supper of the Lamb![122] The Bible says those who get invited to that particular bash are 'blessed' or 'happy'. That is going to be the party to eclipse all parties!

Make no mistake. God is, as Tony Campolo says, 'a party Deity'. If we're going to be like him, then we need to learn how to celebrate life – now! Fun and celebration are not designed to be a post-death experience reserved for the hereafter.

That does not mean that we will run around with streamers, party hats and cheerful grins twenty-six hours of the day. Life is full of ordinary, mundane and sometimes boring and downright painful bits. But as we get to grips with the fact that our Father loves to celebrate, we can learn to 'rejoice in the Lord always'.[123]

The heart of the party: thanksgiving

The celebration began because the boy was safe and sound. Therefore the party was appropriate. (Later the father says, 'We *had* to celebrate.')

Life can have a celebratory feel if we will learn to walk in thanksgiving – and what a striking contrast we shall be to those around us. The noise of the grumblers and complainers in this world sometimes reaches a deafening level. The weather's too hot, or too cold; life's too busy, or too boring. Negativity abounds.

Ask many British people the simple social question, 'How are you?'

'Not too bad.' (I can't bear to say that I'm well, so I'll settle for not as bad as I could be.)

'All right, under the circumstances.' (I'm firmly under

them as well. In fact, my circumstances are practically flattening me.)

'I can't complain.' (One gets the impression that the person would prefer to complain, but can't think of anything at that moment to moan about.)

God calls us to walk in an attitude that is positive and thankful. If you ever wondered about God's direction for your life, this is the will of God for every single one of us.[124]

Why is it then that we have looked upon 'giving thanks' as something that is done only before a meal – and often with a prayer that we've prayed so often that it has lost all sense of real significance? Why can't we give thanks for music, sunshine, friendship, children, laughter, sex and a thousand and one other good things that come from God?

A grateful heart will find it difficult to lounge in self-pity. According to Scripture, a thankful heart will avoid anxiety as well: 'Do not be anxious about anything, but in everything, by prayer and petition, with thanksgiving, present your requests to God. And the peace of God, which transcends all understanding, will guard your hearts and minds in Christ Jesus.'[125]

Be thankful for *answered* prayer too. A lot of us believe in prayer, but fewer believe in *answered prayer*. When God gives us something in response to our requests, we are surprised rather than thankful.

Some years ago tens of thousands of people marched through the City of London for Jesus. They were there to proclaim rather than complain. They celebrated, rebuked principalities and powers, and delivered a letter to the then Prime Minister Mrs Thatcher.

For the next few weeks politicians were swift to make

public comments about Christianity. Mrs Thatcher made a speech on the eve of the march about the need for Christian values in our schools. Opposition leader Neil Kinnock, a member of the Humanist Society, reportedly threw Bible verses across the floor of the House of Commons.

And, perhaps predictably, some Christians said to those who organized the prayer march, 'You don't actually think *your* prayers changed anything, do you?'

Of course they did! Why do we pray, if we expect no response? Is it just that prayer has become the evangelical rosary?

When God responds to our intercession, let's be thankful, and give him the glory (credit) where glory is due.

Celebrating in pain

Jesus wept. Sometimes his followers weep too. Things happen that we don't understand; despite the many answers that the Bible gives, there are many things that are still beyond the reach of our understanding. Sometimes two and two appear to make five.

We used to sing a hymn, 'I'm living on the mountain underneath a cloudless sky.' The only problem with that rather nice sentiment is that there *are* times when the sky is funeral black and it's pouring. A child is dying. A terrible road accident takes place. A faithful Christian (who did tithe) goes bankrupt. It all happens to believers. Is celebration possible during a downpour? Are we to be thankful for everything?

Some years ago a best-selling book was published which taught that we should praise God for everything that happens. Is your daughter a prostitute? Did your grandmother get run over this morning? Is your precious little baby hideously deformed? According to the book, you should thank God for it all. Notice here: thank God *for* it, not *in* it. That's the idea.

If you follow this teaching, then next time your spouse reverses the car over your foot, you are to yell, 'Thank you, Jesus!' at the top of your voice, which, I have to admit, is better than a few other choice phrases that might quickly come to mind.

The whole concept is based on just one verse, which commands us to thank God for everything.[126] The problem is, whenever you take one scripture out of context, you're in trouble.

God is the author of every good and perfect gift, which comes down from the Father of lights,[127] and for all that God does, we must be grateful. But I can't thank God for sin, sexual perversion and murder. I can't believe that the parents of a little child who was brutally raped and strangled are called to thank God *for* that devilish outrage; such an act causes the Lord to weep.

Rather, Scripture invites us to learn to be thankful when we pass through difficulty and agony. Whatever our circumstances, certain facts remain for those of us who walk with God: we are loved, saved, forgiven and cared for. Today may well be very dark, but there really is a better day coming, when we shall see our God face to face.

That's why Paul and Silas were able to sing songs of thanksgiving and praise at midnight in what might have been a condemned cell, for all they knew. They'd been stripped and beaten, they were locked up in stocks, but thankfulness broke out anyway.

141

I really believe that God can and will give us special grace and help to know his closeness during pain. Many have shared how God met with them in a special way during extreme trial. Wendy White was one of nine missionaries who were brutally raped and beaten to death in the Vumba, Zimbabwe, in 1978. An eyewitness who saw the killing shared how, in her final moments, and knowing that death was coming, she cried out to one of her colleagues, 'Don't worry, Phil. They can't kill the soul!' The grace of God was there in the valley of pain. In a sense, celebration broke out even as the bayonet came closer.

We don't have to wait to celebrate until the landscape is clear of pain and difficulty; right now there are reasons to be grateful.

Celebrating together

The father threw the party to say 'thank you', *and* to say 'welcome home' to his long lost son. The joy was not reserved for Father and son alone; friends and neighbours were invited to share the fun.

When you have real friends, you're rich. In America, only one in every five men has a friend. Technology has usurped relationship; you can watch television, rent a film on video, play computer games – all in isolation.

And the result? Desperate loneliness, a fur-lined hell.

T. S. Eliot, expressing the futility of isolation, asked, 'What is life, if we have not life together?'

God has designed the church to fill that friendship vacuum. The early church filled the gap – the people were together, sharing joys, sorrows, resources; a people who loved God and loved one another. Larry Tomczack says, 'The early church drew love-starved pagans like kids to a candy stall!'

The tragedy is that today the church is often too busy with services to have time for friendship, which is very surprising, considering that you don't find one single service in the New Testament – only meetings!

In a sense, we need to abandon our service mentality, which exalts a programme over both God and God's people, and adopt a meeting mentality, so that we can come together and bless God and one another.

Fellowship is designed to be more than a quick handshake during the service, or the bit we do at the end while clutching a cup of tea. Why not serve refreshments *during* the meeting? What about our lives during the rest of the week when there are no 'services' to draw us together? Do we get together (and not only for Bible study and prayer), or is our 'fellowship' limited to close encounters of an evangelical kind as we go in and out of the services?

Of course, some folk prefer to keep Jesus as their 'personal Lord and Saviour' (sounds more like a walkman than a God). American pastor Bruce Larson tells of the day he was confronted by a member of his congregation:

A man came to me and said, 'You know what? I don't like these home groups.'

I said, 'Who cares? You don't have to like them. If you're freezing to death, your best friend would make you get up and walk. It would be more comfortable for you to lay down and die, but a friend makes you do the painful thing so that you might live. A lot of us are naturally shy. We don't want to get involved and share and care, but we

143

do it anyway – it's the route to life. The alternative is death.'[128]

My own love affair with the church began the night I became a Christian. Having been collared by a zealous believer who witnessed to me, I decided that I wanted to meet Jesus for myself. I was invited to go to 'the little room at the back', as the counselling room was discreetly called.

Together with a friend, I sat and listened to the good news for the first time. I was amazed and thrilled as I heard about the God who likes me so much even though he knows all about me!

Time was getting on. There had been the evening service, then a meeting following that (thoughtfully described as the 'after meeting') and now it was about 10pm.

I made my choice – I wanted to know God – and when I got off my knees, having prayed a simple 'sinner's prayer', I knew that something had changed for ever.

Then I opened the door of the counselling room, and got the shock of my life. I thought everyone would have gone home by now, but they had waited to welcome my friend and me into the family of God. I can remember the cheer that went up as we stepped out of that room. The people formed a long line, and we had to walk down that queue, receiving hugs and handshakes and words of welcome as we did. It was so wonderful!

In the counselling room, I started to love Jesus. As I went down the queue, I started to love his church.

No-one had to tell me to go to church from then on. I had to be with these people; they waited for me and welcomed me. (In fact, I met Kay, my wife, when I went down that line!)

We must learn to value friendships above ministry, above money, above everything but God. It's difficult to party alone.

Invest yourself in your church. Go out of your way to welcome. Proverbs says, 'He who would have friends must show himself to be friendly.' Be hospitable! Don't worry if your home isn't as palatial as you'd like. We're called to hospitality, not entertaining.

If you can't afford to have people for a meal, ask them to have coffee, or water! Above all, take the initiative, because the church becomes more loving as you and I take loving steps forward.

When I was a minister, people would occasionally come to me and say, 'Our church isn't friendly enough.'

What was I supposed to do? Wave a magic wand, or sprinkle some secret 'fellowship dust' over the people during the Sunday morning meeting?

The church grows in friendship as you and I grow in friendship. Go for it!

Celebrating: worship

When the first meeting of the Christian church took place on the Day of Pentecost, there were many who mistook it for a party. The sound of celebration was loud enough to draw an enormous crowd, and the apostles had to explain gently that it was too early in the day to be drunk.

As the Holy Spirit came upon the church, the party began, and the words of David were fulfilled: 'Celebrate [God's] abundant goodness, and joyfully sing of [his] righteousness.'[129]

It was A. W. Tozer who mourned that 'worship is the missing jewel of the church'. Over the last twenty years or so, God has been powerfully restoring that priceless gem to the church in Britain. The spirit of celebration is flowing – and it's infectious!

One London-based church that I know is really keen that God should be celebrated and worshipped during Christian weddings. Let's face it, even the most boisterous churches can be tempted to pack their worship away for a wedding. After all, there are lots of people around at weddings who don't know Jesus. There may be a whole row of aunts at the back who might be offended if we dance, or speak in tongues, so let's be safe.

This particular church felt that such a notion was hypocritical. A wedding day should be a celebration, with the Lord Jesus at the centre. So they decided to worship without fear.

During one wedding, the praise and worship had been particularly expressive, with lots of dancing and cheering. Towards the end of the ceremony, the bride and groom went out to sign the register, and one of the church leaders stood, and made a simple evangelistic invitation. He used the worship as an example of what loving God can be like, and then invited those who wanted to respond to Christ to step forward there and then.

The bridegroom's father, mother and brother walked to the front of the church and surrendered their lives to Jesus right in the middle of the wedding. A message was sent in to the bride and groom, telling them to stay where they were and not come out for the wedding march, as their relatives were being counselled!

What a wonderful wedding present. Better than Tupperware any day!

An encounter with a group of partying Christians may be initially a little confusing for a non-Christian, but it's better than stumbling in on the frozen chosen.

The early church had to explain the reason for their party. It was an event that took place because of God. Is it possible that we have allowed the church to die of composure, so that we have no event to offer an explanation for?

Come on and celebrate

We all worship in different ways, but let's start to break out of our fears and inhibitions and worship the Lord as David did – 'with all his might'.[130]

Perhaps that's one reason David was called 'a man after God's own heart' – because he refused to be half-hearted about his God. 'I will not sacrifice to the LORD my God burnt offerings that cost me nothing,' he declared.[131] Worship is about whole-hearted adulation rather than just the singing of a few songs before we listen to the preacher.

However we express ourselves to God, let's give ourselves totally, because God is not just looking for worship. He's looking for worshippers.

I once got a punch in the head during a worship service, and I didn't mind at all. I have a good friend who doesn't just dance when he worships, he *really* dances! I think Mike Morris is incapable of being satisfied with that little charismatic two-step where you hop from one foot to the other like the proverbial cat on hot bricks. When he dances, arms and legs go flailing in every direction.

I remember standing beside Mike once at a large conference. We didn't know each other then, but I was soon introduced. As the worship began, Mike began to dance and, suddenly, whack! One of the flying arms caught me on the side of the head. He was so taken up with giving God his best that he didn't notice that I'd received a good slap in the process.

There are some who refuse to express their worship physically, on the basis that they must be 'in the Spirit'. Some folk talk about 'dancing in the Spirit', which is a term that I find nowhere in the Bible.

The idea seems to be that you are minding your own business during a worship meeting, when suddenly you get mugged by the Holy Spirit, who then forces you to do things you wouldn't dream of doing if you were in control of yourself. Normally quiet and reserved people are transformed into worthy rivals for John Travolta when God takes over – at least, that's the theory.

Why is it that we talk only about 'dancing in the Spirit', as opposed to clapping, or kneeling, or lifting our hands in the Spirit?

Perhaps one reason is that it would take something of a divine earthquake to make some of us dance!

The fact is that *all* worship should be in the Spirit; that means in flow with what God is doing, and pleasing to the Holy Spirit. To be in the Spirit doesn't mean that we lose control of ourselves. 'The spirits of prophets are subject to the control of prophets,'[132] says the scripture. That means we are in control. God may encourage us, woo us, draw us, even overpower us – but we worship because we *choose* to worship, as an act of the will. The Holy Spirit moves as he is welcomed.

God has consistently honoured the will of human beings from the beginning – we choose to be saved, we choose to serve, we choose to worship. Love is a choice. We are humans, not robots in the Spirit.

God give us a party feel in the church again!

Celebration: enjoying the moments

The church father Irenaeus wrote: 'The glory of God is man fully alive.'

Sometimes it's good to do things in life just for the sake of it. It would be a mistake to suggest that parties are only functional, held simply for purpose alone. Parties are often thrown just for the sheer fun of it.

Creation reveals a God at play, an artist who splashes colour and variety around the cosmic canvas.

Sadly, Christians are often the most driven people around. There have been times when I have felt withered by a sermon on 'Making the best use of time'; the suggestion is that everything must have a purpose, the hour is short, no time can be wasted. Only the truly useful can be justified.

Those who try to live purposeful and useful lives twenty-four hours a day will, in my opinion, die prematurely and before many of their purposes have been realized. To be driven like this will cause a state of paranoia where we find it impossible to relax. Tim Hansel sums up the feeling with the title of his excellent book: *When I Relax I Feel Guilty!* When we are always living in order to achieve something, we miss out on life itself. As Hugh Prather puts it:

I want to be doing things to be doing them
I don't want to do nice things for people so that I
  will be 'nice'

I don't want to work to make money
I want to work to work.
Today I don't want to live *for*
I want to live.[133]

Perhaps we are the victims of our own Protestant work
ethic, where the greatest goodness is ascribed to those
who work the hardest. We need to learn to play again, to
do things just for the sake of doing them, to be a little
crazy every now and again.

There are many things that I remember with affection
from my childhood, but for some reason, my best
memory is that feeling I got while out camping with
my brother. I can vividly recall lying there, in the snug
warmth of my sleeping bag, listening to the torrential
rain cascading on to the canvas. The feeling of warmth
and security while all was wet and cold outside was
wonderful.

Do we rush through life at such a speed, and miss all
manner of treasures in the blur of it all? Gems like the
smell of freshly baked bread, or the haze that appears on
the road ahead on a really hot day, or the fragrance of
freshly mown grass?

I don't think that you have to be particularly 'arty' to
enjoy these gifts. I enjoy art, but I confess that I have
been utterly confused on more than one occasion by a
poem or a dance or mime in church. Everyone else was
nodding and murmuring approval and appreciation,
while I was left wondering what on earth the point was
in it all! (I have a theory that quite a few people are as
artistically thick as I am, but to admit it is to appear
stupid.)

Nigel Goodwin often talks about Christians being

called to *be* rather than to *do*. The Pharisees were good at doing, but had never learned how to be, so their doing was false and vain. Elijah was good at raising the dead and commanding fire to fall from heaven, but had never learned to relax, rest and eat properly. The result was a suicidal prophet praying for death in a cave.[134]

Perhaps you would complain that you are just too busy to play.

Who had a more important agenda on earth than the Lord Jesus? He was constantly surrounded by need and opportunity, but said to his disciples, 'Come apart and rest a while.' Admittedly, the vacation wasn't too successful, because the crowds found out where the Lord and his disciples were having their day off, but the attempt was made. It has been said that if we refuse to 'come apart' then before long we will come apart . . .

Recreation provides that opportunity for re-creation that we all so desperately need. That's why God thought of the Sabbath principle in the first place.

Wilfred Peterson wrote this prayer:

Slow me down, Lord.

Ease the pounding of my heart by the quieting of my mind.

Steady my hurried pace with a vision of the eternal reach of time.

Give me, amid the confusion of the day, the calmness of the everlasting hills.

Break the tensions of my nerves and muscles with the soothing music of the singing streams that live in my memory.

Teach me the art of taking minute vacations – of slowing down to look at a flower, to chat with a friend, to pat a dog, to smile at a child, to read a few lines from a good book.

Slow me down, Lord, and inspire me to send my roots deep into the soil of life's enduring values, that I may grow toward my greater destiny.

Remind me each day that the race is not always to the swift; that there is more to life than increasing its speed.

Let me look upward to the towering oak and know that it grew great and strong because it grew slowly and well.

The God of the parable is a God who celebrates life – not a heavenly chairperson, a time-and-motion being.

With thanksgiving, friendship, worship and play, we can make our own response to a call that rings out now, and will continue for ever: 'Let's party!'

III

THE ELDER BROTHER

III

chapter eight

Big brother . . . the new prodigal

So they began to celebrate. Meanwhile, the older son was in the field. When he came near the house, he heard music and dancing. So he called one of the servants and asked him what was going on. 'Your brother has come,' he replied, 'and your father has killed the fattened calf because he has him back safe and sound.'

The older brother became angry and refused to go in. So his father went out and pleaded with him. But he answered his father, 'Look! All these years I've been slaving for you and never disobeyed your orders. Yet you never gave me even a young goat so I could celebrate with my friends. But when this son of yours who has squandered your property with prostitutes comes home, you kill the fattened calf for him!'

'My son,' the father said, 'you are always with me, and everything I have is yours. But we had to celebrate and be glad, because this brother of yours was dead and is alive again; he was lost and is found.'

The party was in full swing, and everybody (with the notable exception of the fattened calf) was happy. The music and the sound of dancing could be heard from quite a distance.

Outside the house, a man stood alone, listening. No smile rested upon his face. Suddenly he summoned one of the servants and demanded an explanation. What was all the fuss about?

The answer served only to heighten his anger. His features twisted with rage, his fists clenched knuckle-white and he spat out a command: 'I want to see the master. Out here. Now!'

The servant scurried off quickly to find the head of the house . . .

The last five or ten minutes had been rather difficult for the Pharisees who listened from the back of the crowd. They were shocked to the core as Jesus described the God who loved sinners and welcomed them with open arms. But they'd seen nothing yet. Now the spotlight focused fully upon them as Jesus introduced the third major character in the story: the elder brother.

I've heard many talks and sermons based on this parable, and often this final part of the story isn't even mentioned. Everything ends with the Prodigal coming home. But the concluding seven verses are vital and key in the teaching of Jesus. As the elder brother arrives, the Lord uses him to unmask something as heinous as sin itself: religion.

The enemy of the Spirit: religion

Those who are careless about their Christianity invariably get entangled in sin – and those who are careful and keen often get snared by religion.

We begin our Christian lives with a loving intensity, thrilled with God and committed to our relationship with him. Sadly, that fervour can degenerate into a mere religiosity; we are passionate about our doctrines, opinions and traditions, and lose sight of the living God in the process. The zeal is still burning, but it is a religious zeal.

Religiosity is a subtle enemy as well: it appears to be very pious and devout, but despite the disguise, religion is the sworn enemy of the Spirit of God.

It was the Pharisees and Sadducees, the religious experts, who hounded and heckled Jesus – not the sinners. The irreligious listened and often received the truth with joy, but the religious tried to catch him out with awkward questions. They were the ones who tried to put division between Jesus and his disciples.[135] It was the Pharisees who, even in the early stages of our Lord's ministry, began to plot how they might kill him.[136] At what seemed like every turn, they opposed what God was doing, finding fault and undermining the work of the Messiah.

They scrutinized Jesus and tried to make small issues large. When he and his disciples omitted the ceremonial hand-washing before meals (which was a matter of tradition, not law),[137] the religious made a predictable fuss.

No wonder he called them blind. Great miracles had failed to open their eyes. They explained the signs away by accusing the Son of God of being filled with demonic power![138]

One would have thought that the raising of Lazarus, formerly a stinking corpse, would have helped them to understand. But though they acknowledged the miraculous sign, they immediately held a committee meeting. The first item on the agenda was the proposed assassination of Jesus.

And it was the chief priests and the elders who whipped the crowd into a bloodthirsty frenzy when the people were asked to choose one man for mercy; Jesus and Barabbas were on the voting paper.

The religious leaders voted for Barabbas, formed a political support group, and succeeded in getting the criminal released and Jesus executed.

And even during his last seconds on the cross, Jesus had to put up with the taunts of religious leaders, who acted as satanic cheerleaders: 'He saved others,' they said, 'but he can't save himself . . . Let God rescue him now.'[139]

No wonder Jesus warned his disciples to beware of religion. His instruction concerning the teaching of the Pharisees and Sadducees was simple: stay away from it.[140]

Religion and religious people persistently snapped at his heels as he went about living the good news.

And nothing's changed. Religion is still the major opponent of the Spirit of God. It opposes change and renewal; it criticizes freedom and spontaneity in worship, and screams with discomfort when traditionalism is challenged. It is religion that hollers when the Holy Spirit does something fresh and creative, and that wants to lock men and women up in the dreary dungeons of legalism.

Perhaps that's why the word 'religion' is used only six times in the New Testament . . . and most of the time it's used in a negative sense.

The pagan Festus, in his conversation with King Agrippa,[141] described Paul's Christian faith as his 'religion' but in the next chapter Paul uses the word 'religion' to describe his condition as a Pharisee *before* meeting Jesus.[142]

Elsewhere both Paul and James use the term some-what negatively: people 'should learn first of all to put their religion into practice', Paul advises Timothy.[143] James uses the term three times to describe the worth-lessness of mere religion. He tells the religious to put their actions where their theories are.[144]

The prodigal in the pew

The arrival of the elder brother is more than a tidy little postscript to end the story neatly. He is the lone protester outside the party, and an ironic transformation has taken place, for a new prodigal has emerged.

The elder son never left home. He worked hard, and could boast that he had avoided the overt debauchery of his kid brother. But he is now the new prodigal. He is miles from the pigs, but miles from the father's heart as well.

Religion can cause us to become prodigals in the pew: our bodies in the church building once or twice a week, our behaviour fairly conservative, but our hearts in the far country.

We need to examine this big brother closely, and strip off the sanctimonious veneer of religion as we do so. Religion is just like sin – it needs to be exposed for what it really is.

The heart of religion: self

God is never to be found at the heart of religion. Self, in the form of self-righteousness, pride and bigotry, is invariably at the centre. Jesus taught that the Pharisees were full of self-indulgence.[145]

'Look here!' yells the brother to his father – and then proceeds to try to tell Dad what he should and shouldn't do in his own household!

Religious people still try to boss God around in his own kingdom today.

I heard of a lady who went up to the late David Watson after one of his meetings, and announced, 'Now look here, Mr Watson, we don't want anything super-natural in *our* church!' Such an example seems almost too absurd to be true, but religious control is a major problem in many churches today. The Holy Spirit begins something new in the local church, and so change (which is here to stay when the Holy Spirit is in control) is inevitable. Suddenly the sound of murmuring voices can be heard: 'I don't like what's happening in our church. It's not like it used to be.'

Stop right there! Whose church? The church belongs to Jesus. He died to redeem this outfit; the title deeds are in his possession. Who are we to tell God what to do? As Isaiah said, 'Does the clay say to the potter, "What are you making?"'[146]

The Pharisees didn't like what Jesus was doing in healing the sick and raising the dead, and they frantically tried to harness and bind the very Son of God. Read through the gospel of Matthew and you'll see how hard they worked at it.

And what happens when religious people find themselves unable to control the divine agenda? They change church . . . or crucify someone.

I used to live in a relatively small community in southern Oregon. The population was probably no more than 50,000 people, yet there were over 100 churches in that town. Every time God began to move, arguments would break out, the pastor would be fired and churches would split.

If revival is ever to come, then we must lay ourselves open to the as yet unknown divine agenda. God has this recurring habit of being God – and he won't change or abdicate for you or me.

Religion: a small-minded, petty attitude

'You never gave me even a young goat,' bleated the son.

We must not think that religion confines itself to weighty issues. Often it will rear its head in order to scream about minor matters. The elder brother was unable to see the wonderful truth that his family was complete again; he couldn't see past his own sense of discomfort at the apparent unfairness of the situation.

Of course, it's rank immaturity. Little children are fond of using the phrase, 'It's not fair!' If one child is given a bar of chocolate, the other must have a bar of exactly the same size and/or value. But it isn't only the tots who cry over non-issues. Adults are rather good at playing spiritual Trivial Pursuit as well. The Pharisees played the game when Jesus healed a man with a withered hand on the Sabbath.[147] A deformed man was gloriously healed, the kingdom of God broke out in power, and the religious crowd screamed, 'But he healed him on God's day off!' Petty thinking caused them to focus on the insignificant and to ignore the magnificent.

One church I know was experiencing a significant renewal in worship. A fresh sense of encounter with God was felt as the people gave themselves to praise and thanksgiving with effort and enthusiasm. But some folk complained that they were thinking of leaving the church. (What they actually said was that God was leading them elsewhere. God often gets the blame for our fickle immaturity.)

Later, the reason for the exodus became clear. 'We are going to another church,' they said, 'because we stand up too long during the worship time.'

Perhaps I'm stupid or naïve, but I have a better solution. If your legs get tired during extended worship times, then don't leave the church, shatter relationships, destroy growth and end your effectiveness in the body. Why not just sit down?

The ability of the religious to make mountains out of molehills is legendary. I heard of another church that split over a cake. A chocolate cake sale was held to raise funds for the church building. One of the congregation (who had been a member for about 300 years and should have known better) baked a cake and brought it along on the day of the sale. But, horror of horrors, no one bought her cake!

Hell hath no fury like a woman who baked a cake which no-one wanted to eat, so she got all her relatives together who attended the church, and poured out her complaint. They were furious, and split the church, and formed their own! Perhaps they called it the First Reformed Assembly of the Blessed Holy Cake.

'You didn't give me even a goat, so there,' was the attitude of the aggrieved older brother. Where religion is in charge, petty trivia become important. Like the Hebrews who complained to Moses that they were without cucumbers or leeks, but conveniently forgot how they'd recently walked through a parted sea and been delivered from infanticide and slavery, the religious see only that which causes them personal discomfort.

The self-righteousness of religion

The elder brother had a problem with his dad's theology – as far as he was concerned, grace was too good.

How could Dad throw a welcome party for a sinner like the Prodigal? 'You've killed the fattened calf . . . for *him!*'

The grace of God offends the religious heart, because grace strips us of any ability to buy Father's favour. So we develop a legalistic system of works-orientated Christianity. Yes, we're saved by grace through faith, but kept by legalism through sweat!

Legalism defined

We need to define the word 'legalism', because there is a danger that we can brand anything and everything that is habitual or born of discipline as legalistic.

An example of this could be the practice of prayer before meals. Saying grace can become a repetitious and faintly superstitious practice that is totally devoid of meaning, and therefore legalistic. On the other hand, giving thanks to God with a genuine attitude of real gratitude before eating a meal may be habitual but full of life none the less. My fear is that in our desire to avoid religiosity we overreact and throw the proverbial baby out with the bath water. We reject anything that demands consistent discipline on the basis of not wanting to be legalistic.

Legalism: traditionalism

'You nullify the word of God for the sake of your tradition,' Jesus said to the Pharisees.[148]

There's a difference between tradition and traditionalism. Some of our traditions are useful, and rich in meaning. I traditionally take a shower every morning. My family and friends are glad! I have friends who are filled with the Holy Spirit who worship in a more traditional setting than my own, and how the Lord is blessing them!

It's tradition*alism* – where God wants to take us in a direction but 'the way we've always done things' prevents us from following him – that's the problem. When we refuse to allow God to move, and cling to our predictable patterns instead, we commit idolatry, for there can be only one Lord in the church.

The local church can avoid traditionalism by being brave enough to ask 'Why?' about everything she does. *Why* do we meet twice on Sunday/sing three hymns/sing 300 choruses/have a preach at the end/sit in rows/sit in circles/have communion every week?

We might find good reason for what we do, but let's at least be brave enough to ask the questions anyway.

Legalism: looking good on the surface

Imitation is big business. I once saw a label sewn into a coat stating 'genuine imitation leather'.

Legalism offers a veneer; it is plastic 'genuine imitation' Christianity. Legalism requires me to change my outward behaviour, but not my heart or mind. Because my behaviour fits in with the local set of rules, I look quite impressive. The problem is, I may be able to keep up the act on Sundays and when I'm around other Christians, but inside, in my heart and mind, nothing's really changed.

True Christianity is about a change of heart that leads to a change of behaviour: we are 'transformed by the renewing of our minds'.

I mention this first because it was religious external-ism that really angered the Lord Jesus. 'Everything they do is done for men to see,' he said of the Pharisees and Sadducees.[149] Their whole lives were consumed by a passion to impress. Phylacteries (little boxes containing verses of Scripture) were worn on their foreheads and arms. Prayer shawls were lengthened as a sign of importance and piety. They relished occupying the best seats in the synagogues, and were totally committed to ecclesiastical title power: everyone had to call them 'Rabbi'.

Jesus called them 'dirty mugs' (well, cups actually), clean on the outside but full of greed inside. He called them 'graves': clean and white without, dead men's bones within.

The grace of God means that we are called to walk in a daily process of *having out minds renewed*, and then we shall be truly transformed.[150] As we are filled with the Spirit and fed on the Scripture, as we walk in friendship and accountability in God's church, so real change can take place. Children of the Father can be transformed; slaves of religion have to sweat it out.

The elder brother looked fine on the outside, but he was actually acting more like a slave than a son, and his heart had burned over the years with resentment towards his father. Notice that the elder brother never once used the word 'father'.

Contrast that with the first words of the returning younger brother earlier: 'Father, I have sinned.'

It's ironic. The younger brother came home and asked to be made a slave, and was restored to sonship; the elder brother never left home, but had lived in slavery for years.

Legalism: someone else's list of rules

The Pharisees were masters at making up extra religious rules. They built fences around the law, and added regulations that were designed to keep you as far away from lawbreaking as possible.

An example of this would be in the area of pride. Obviously God resists the proud and exalts the humble. To make sure that this was followed in daily life, the Pharisees developed rules about exactly how much you could compliment a bride on her wedding day.

No woman was allowed to look into a mirror on the Sabbath on the basis that, if she did, she might see a grey hair, pull it out, and thus work on the Lord's day!

Every area of life seemed to have a tangle of regulations attached to it that had no origin in the heart of God. No wonder Jesus told the Pharisees that they were guilty of 'shut[ting] the kingdom of heaven in men's faces'.[151]

I'm amazed at the fences which still stand today, and many of them are grounded in neither Scripture nor logic. I know, for example, many Christians who wouldn't be seen dead in the cinema – they wait until the film comes out on video. I'm not arguing for or against the cinema – some might feel that most of the material Hollywood turns out is unhelpful, and that's fine. What I am asking for is some logic and consistency.

Sometimes the fences are so ridiculous that total absurdity results. I met some lovely older women in a church in Texas who shared with me about how things used to be back in 'the bad old days'. With a twinkle in their eyes, they told me about the day an evangelist came to preach. He declared that it was a sin for the women in the church to shave their legs! The result? Dozens of pious gorillas running around town, being 'hairy unto the Lord'!

Of course, I have to honour the women who obeyed this ridiculous teaching. Yes, they should have searched their Bibles and known better, but I'm sure many of them did what they did because they wanted to honour God. The real culprit and villain of this illustration is the preacher who came up with the crazy idea in the first place. Jesus rebuked the Pharisees for making the rules, not the people who did their best to follow those rules.

There are times when the legalist will actually exalt the rules *above* Scripture. A friend of mine comes from a background where the teaching that the bread and wine of communion are 'only bread and only wine' is rigidly taught. On one occasion he decided to test the reality of the doctrine by chewing on a piece of communion bread during his sermon. Surely, if the congregation really believed that it was 'just bread' and that it had no special value or intrinsic holiness of its own, they wouldn't be offended . . . would they?

The nuclear explosion that followed was proof of the fact that legalism had strangled the truth for those folk. He was made to feel that a major act of desecration had taken place.

Of course, there is something attractive about following the local rule book. It means that you don't have to think, read Scripture, and ask God yourself about how you should live. Legalism is actually laziness with a religious overlay.

Grace allows us to live out the truth in the power of the Spirit. Legalism demands that we follow human ideas (often false and unbiblical ideas) in the power of fear and flesh.

I know where I'd rather live!

Legalism: principles matter more than people

I've noticed that religious people are often really concerned about their principles, doctrines and opinions, and people cease to matter. The elder brother, referring to the Prodigal, says, 'This son of yours . . . ' He's so concerned for his own protection, and for 'the cause of righteousness', that he actually forgets that the Prodigal is not only the son of his father, he is also his long-lost brother! Gently, the father reminds him in his reply: 'This *brother of yours* was dead and is alive again.' Do we forget who our brothers and sisters are?

When I was a young pastor of a growing but small church, I invited one of our denominational leaders to come and preach. The sermon was good, but not quite what some of our folk would have expected. At the end of the meeting, one of our congregation, who had been walking with us for a couple of years, came storming up to me as I stood at the door, and shouted, 'My family and I will never darken the doors of this church again.' Then, with a word of insult to me personally, he stormed off. He later apologized, but that family never did come back. And all because they disagreed with a couple of lines from a guest speaker's sermon.

The elder brother not only forgot who his brother was, but he had a poor memory for the truth as well! 'This son of yours . . . has squandered your property with prostitutes.'

Now hold on right there. Who said anything about prostitutes? The elder brother hadn't even been into the party to speak to anybody, and the narrative mentions nothing about prostitutes. It's the elder brother himself who introduces this juicy little rumour as he seeks to destroy and slander his brother.

The fact is that religious people can be the most terrible gossips and rumour-mongers. That's why James warns those who think they're rather advanced in spiritual matters: 'If anyone considers himself religious and yet does not keep a tight rein on his tongue, he deceives himself and his religion is worthless.'[152]

I once illustrated this during a meeting, and a number of people nearly suffered a heart attack. I stood up and announced that God had told me there was a member present who had caused great distress and dissension, and that I was going to expose that member publicly. As you will imagine, the place went deathly quiet. People gripped their chairs in terror as I continued. I said, 'In a few seconds everyone will know who it is. This member must be exposed, here – and now.'

There was a man who had been playing the piano who looked more and more worried as I went on. In the end, he got up and sat underneath the piano, he was so terrified!

I waited until I felt that the collective blood pressure of the congregation could stand it no more. 'The time has come – all will now be revealed. The name of this member that has caused trouble around here is . . . the tongue, which the Bible says is an unruly member.'

A great sigh of relief swept across the crowd, and a resurrection took place behind the piano!

But isn't it the truth? The Pharisees looked wonderful, but their mouths were full of poisonous venom.

Refuse to pass rumours around, and refuse to believe

the worst about your brother or sister. Demand proof! If someone tells you a slanderous story, why not suggest that you and the gossip go to see the one who is being gossiped about immediately, so that the truth can be clarified?

Religion and legalism exalt principle . . . and punch people.

Legalism: good works or good God?

The elder brother was a true legalist, because he was convinced that he really did *deserve* a party. He had a great pride in himself. 'All these years I've been slaving for you and never disobeyed your orders. Yet you never gave me . . .'

Those who live under grace are aware that they deserve nothing and have been given everything. They should get hell, but instead are granted heaven. Human pride has to flee in the face of such a towering love.

Legalists quietly believe that in the end God will open heaven because of their hard work and obedience.

Paul is a great example of someone who had been driven for too long by proud legalism. In fact, he declared that he looked upon all that religious stuff in the past as 'dung'. (Isn't it interesting how the strongest language from Paul and from the Lord Jesus is reserved for cursed religiosity?)

Delivered from that way of life, he was able to say, 'The love of Christ constrains me.'

That's why he obeyed.

That's why he suffered.

That's why he endured.

To earn love? To be able to say, 'All these years I've been slaving for you, Lord. Now I deserve a crown'?

No! All that he did was because he had received amazing love.

The true tyranny of legalism is that it warps our understanding of God. Rather than being a Father to us, he becomes a slave-driver, a heavenly taskmaster who insists that we keep the rules in order to retain his love, rather than walk in integrity because we're thrilled with his love.

That's why the father in the story began his response with the words, 'My son . . .'

The father was thrilled that his young son was home, but he loved the older brother just as much, and quickly reminded him: 'You're no slave; you're my son.' A reminder is given about the privileges of sonship as well: 'You are always with me, and everything I have is yours.'

Religion, like sin, is robbery. It robs us of our joy as sons and daughters of God, forcing us to feel and act like slaves.

It robs us of the joy of being able to find out how God would have us live, as we settle for someone else's rule book.

It robs us of true, enduring friendship: relationships last only as long as others agree with our religious principles.

In short, religion leaves us standing outside in the cold, while others enjoy the Father's party. Make no mistake about it: this parable should be called 'the parable of the prodigal sons', for there were two of them: one lost to sin, now restored; the other lost to religion, but a prodigal still.

Epilogue

So his father went out and pleaded with him.

The story ends with the father outside for the second time that day, pleading with his elder son, begging him to come in and join the party. He explained his actions and affirmed his son, but Jesus ends the story without telling us the outcome.

Did the elder brother go in to the warmth and joy of the house, welcome his brother, and begin to enjoy the celebration? Or did he stay outside, stubborn in the cold?

We are left with the image of a man with his hands on his waist, considering his response.

Perhaps Jesus wanted his listeners in the crowd that day to write their own ending to the story. Would they hear the invitation from the heart of Father God, lay aside their sin and their religion, and enter into a party? Or would they stay outside?

We have to write our own ending to the story too. To each and every one of us, religious and sinner alike, there is a personal invitation, one that demands a response.

The initials RSVP are included: Respond, if you please.

Notes

1. Richard Foster, *Freedom of Simplicity* (Harper & Row, 1981).
2. K. Hagin, *I Believe in Visions* (Faith Library, 1984), p. 124.
3. Reported by Andrew Brandon in *Health and Wealth* (Kingsway, 1987), p. 72, where he attributes the quote to Fred Price in his book *How to Obtain Strong Faith* (Harrison House, Tulsa, OK), p. 28.
4. Luke 3:14.
5. Philippians 4:12a.
6. Philippians 4:12b–13.
7. Philippians 4:10.
8. 1 Corinthians 16:1.
9. 1 Timothy 6:6.
10. 1 Timothy 6:10.
11. James 2:1.
12. 1 Timothy 6:17.
13. 1 Timothy 6:18–19.
14. Luke 12:15.
15. Ecclesiastes 2:3.
16. Ecclesiastes 2:9.
17. Paul Tournier, *The Adventure of Living*.
18. Tim Hansel, *When I Relax I Feel Guilty* (David C. Cook, 1979).
19. Ecclesiastes 12:8.
20. 2 Corinthians 11:23–27.
21. Philippians 4:12–13.
22. Exodus 3:12.
23. Joshua 1:5; Jeremiah 1:8.
24. Matthew 28:20.
25. Hebrews 13:5.
26. Tim Hansel, *When I Relax I Feel Guilty*, p. 84.
27. John 15:5.
28. Matthew 6:33.
29. Matthew 6:11.
30. 2 Corinthians 9:7.
31. Acts 20:35.
32. Tim Hansel, *When I Relax I Feel Guilty*.
33. John 8:44.
34. Genesis 3:6.
35. 2 Corinthians 11:14.
36. Adrian Plass, *Clearing Away the Rubbish* (Kingsway, 1988).
37. John 10:10.
38. James 1:17.

39. Leviticus 11:7.
40. Genesis 1:27.
41. 2 Corinthians 2:10–11.
42. 1 Corinthians 4:10.
43. 2 Corinthians 7:10.
44. Luke 22:33.
45. Luke 22:55.
46. W. E. Vine, *Vine's Dictionary of New Testament Words* (McDonald).
47. Author unable to trace source.
48. Romans 14:12.
49. Luke 19:8.
50. 1 Timothy 2:5.
51. James 5:16.
52. Matthew 3:6.
53. Acts 19:18.
54. Gerald Coates, *What on Earth Is this Kingdom?* (Kingsway, 1983).
55. Nick Cuthbert, *God Is My Father* (Kingsway).
56. Luke 11:1.
57. Luke 15:1.
58. *Prosdechomai*, see *Vine's Dictionary of New Testament Words*.
59. James Hastings (ed.), *Dictionary of Christ and the Gospels* (T. and T. Clark, 1909), vol. II, p. 353.
60. Deuteronomy 32:6; Psalm 68:5.
61. Wisdom 2:16.
62. James Bousset, *The Religion of Judaism*, p. 65. Quoted in Hastings, *Dictionary of Christ and the Gospels*.
63. Matthew 9:36.
64. John 11:1–12.
65. Luke 7:13.
66. Zephaniah 3:17.
67. John 11:35.
68. *Vine's Dictionary of New Testament Words*.
69. Romans 15:4.
70. Matthew 25:23.
71. Hebrews 12:6.
72. Romans 8:16.
73. Romans 8:15.
74. Galatians 4:6.
75. Galatians 5:25.
76. 1 Corinthians 14:4.
77. 2 Samuel 6.
78. 1 Samuel 18:21.
79. 1 Samuel 25:44.
80. 2 Samuel 3:14.
81. 2 Samuel 6:23.
82. John 17:3.
83. A. W. Tozer, *The Pursuit of God* (Kingsway, 1982), p. 17.
84. Luke 3:22.
85. Philippians 3:10.
86. Psalm 63:1.
87. Romans 8:26.
88. Galatians 5:12.
89. Romans 7:15.
90. 1 Corinthians 9:27.
91. 2 Timothy 1:7.
92. David Watson, *Discipleship* (Hodder and Stoughton, 1981), p. 130.
93. Revelation 12:10.
94. Matthew 4:3.
95. 1 John 1:9.
96. Acts 10:11.
97. Acts 10:15.

98. Mark 12:38.
99. Galatians 5:11.
100. Exodus 3:5.
101. Joshua 5:15.
102. Mark 1:7.
103. Psalm 3:3.
104. Genesis 41:42.
105. Esther 3:10.
106. Jude 9.
107. James 4:7.
108. 1 John 4:4.
109. Revelation 12:11.
110. Exodus 12:13.
111. 1 John 1:7.
112. Revelation 12:11.
113. 1 John 3:2.
114. Romans 8:37.
115. Philippians 4:8.
116. 2 Corinthians 10:5.
117. Zephaniah 3:17.
118. Luke 15:10.
119. Deuteronomy 14:26.
120. Luke 7:34.
121. Matthew 22:2–4.
122. Revelation 19:9.
123. Philippians 4:4.
124. 1 Thessalonians 5:18.
125. Philippians 4:6.
126. Ephesians 5:20.
127. James 1:17.
128. Bruce Larson, *Wind and Fire*.
129. Psalm 145:7.
130. 2 Samuel 6:14.
131. 2 Samuel 24:24.
132. 1 Corinthians 14:32.
133. Hugh Prather, *Notes to Myself*.
134. 1 Kings 19.
135. Matthew 9:11.
136. Matthew 12:14.
137. Matthew 15:1–2.
138. Matthew 12:24.
139. Matthew 27:42–43.
140. Matthew 16:12.
141. Acts 25:19.
142. Acts 26:5.
143. 1 Timothy 5:4.
144. James 1:26–27.
145. Matthew 23:25.
146. Isaiah 45:9.
147. Matthew 12:9–14.
148. Matthew 15:6.
149. Matthew 23:5.
150. Romans 12:2.
151. Matthew 23:13.
152. James 1:26.

Jeff Lucas
Revelation Church, PO Box 58, Chichester, West Sussex, PO19 2UD, England.
USA office: PO Box 1144, Albany, Oregon 97321, USA